Praise ᴜₒᵣ

THE ROAD TO HOME OWNERSHIP

A Canadian Buyer's Blueprint

"Packed with humour, relatable scenarios, and insightful tips, this guide makes navigating the world of mortgages, down-payments, and property hunting informative and fun. Readers are gently guided through the overwhelming process of buying a home in Canada. Brijpaul masterfully blends storytelling with practical advice, creating an entertaining and educational resource. Whether you're a buyer or simply curious about the different aspects of Real Estate, this practical read is your perfect starting point."

Dhaman P. Kissoon, BA(Econs.) BA (Law) LLB.
Adjunct Professor (Queen's Faculty Law)

"The Road To Homeownership should be a must for every buyer. Every stage of the process is eloquently described in detail, including possible pitfalls in a home purchase and how to circumvent them. The brilliance of coining this process as a story, makes it so much more inviting as it explains in simple language, the questions and answers of every aspect of the journey."

Dr Ken Singh BA,CITT,MCIT,(Hons . Dr of Laws)

"This book masterfully navigates the complexities of the real estate market with a blend of engaging storytelling, practical advice, and relatable humour. Through the experiences of two recent immigrants navigating Toronto's housing scene, author Jay Brijpaul offers invaluable insights into the home-buying journey. From understanding financing options, navigating cultural nuances, and dealing with unexpected challenges, this book provides a warm and informative companion for anyone embarking on their Canadian homeownership adventure."

—Simone Jennifer Smith—
Chief Correspondent, Toronto Caribbean Newspaper

ALSO BY JAY BRIJPAUL

- *Wealth—Through Real Estate Investing*
- *Articles in Indo Caribbean World and Toronto Caribbean Newspaper*

THE ROAD TO HOME OWNERSHIP

A Canadian Buyer's Blueprint

By

Jay Brijpaul, BSc, FRI

MiddleRoad | Publishers

www.middleroadpublishers.ca

Making Literature See The Light Of Day

Library and Archives Canada Cataloguing in Publication

Brijpaul, Jay, Author

The Road To Home Ownership/ A Canadian Buyer's Blueprint

ISBN 978-1-990765-63-6 (softcover)

Editor: Ken Puddicombe www.kenpud.wordpress.com

Cover Design by Kathryn Lagerquist

Kathryn.lagerquist@gmail.com

"The bottom line: investing in real estate is smart because property is tangible. People always have, and always will, need shelter. This means it is very unlikely that our need for shelter (i.e.: buying or renting homes) will ever go away."
**—Kathy Fettke, Co-Founder and Co-CEO—
of *RealWealth***
Real Estate Investing Simplified

DEDICATION

I have heartfelt gratitude to my clients, whose daily inspiration has been a beacon of light in my journey. With immense joy, I present this book as a humble gift to your children, a testament to the shared dreams and hopes that fuel our future.

THE ROAD TO HOME OWNERSHIP
A Canadian Buyer's Blueprint
EDITOR'S NOTE

While this book offers valuable insight into the Real Estate industry, it is not meant to be *the* solution for achieving wealth.

Jay Brijpaul has laid out his approach in simple, easy-to-follow steps, based on his cumulative thirty years-knowledge of Real Estate in Canada. With this knowledge has come experience that has allowed him to excel and be one of the top practitioners in his field.

The principles espoused by the author, apart from the tax implications which differ from jurisdiction to jurisdiction, hold true for any free-market real-estate environment. While readers will find valuable tips for achieving financial independence and security through real estate investment, the author and publisher accept no responsibility and will not be held liable for investments that don't meet readers' expectations.

Ken Puddicombe, CPA, CMA	Jay Brijpaul BSc, FRI
Editor	Author

www.middleroadpublishers.ca

ACKNOWLEDGMENTS

Every chapter in this book is crafted to enlighten, infused with humour and engaging dialogues. I sincerely thank my daughter, Anjie, whose unwavering assistance and encouragement were invaluable. To my son, Akash, despite your demanding schedule, your thoughtful reviews and insights enriched this work profoundly. Videsh and Kavita, your steadfast support and motivation have been pillars of strength. To the love of my life, Nan, your constant support has been my anchor.

A special acknowledgment to my editor, Ken Puddicombe, for his invaluable suggestions.

Table of Contents

FOREWORD

During the height of the pandemic, when bidding wars were fierce, and home prices soared, a family finally achieved their dream: buying their first home. It was not easy. They poured their savings into a modest townhome in Mississauga, stretching their budget to outbid competitors. Their realtor advised them to pay over $200,000 above the asking price to secure the home—but it was worth it— or so they believed.

At first, everything seemed manageable. Interest rates were at a record low, making their monthly payments reasonable. Life in their new home felt fantastic. But as the years passed, the financial landscape shifted. When it came time to renew their mortgage, their payments skyrocketed. Their townhome, part of a condominium complex and not freehold, carried steep maintenance fees that only added to their financial burden.

Their savings dwindled. Every month became a struggle to keep up with the bills. Then, an even more significant challenge arose—one of the homeowners fell seriously ill. The loss of income pushed them further into hardship.

Selling seemed the only way out, but the market had turned against them. Similar homes were selling for $200,000 less than what they had paid. With closing costs factored in, selling would leave them with a devastating $250,000 shortfall. Worse still, two family members had co-signed their mortgage, meaning that if they defaulted, their financial troubles would extend beyond their household.

What was once this family's most significant milestone had now become their heaviest burden. They had worked hard, saved diligently, and followed what they believed was the right path to homeownership—only to find themselves drowning in debt.

Imagine undertaking a long, complex, and arduous journey without a map. The journey to buying a first home is similar. Many people usually start by asking close friends and acquaintances for guidance. However, people give advice based on their ever-changing personal experiences which may not necessarily apply to your situation. Prospective buyers may also choose to do their research, but understanding real estate jargon can sometimes be like learning a new language. It is very easy to get overwhelmed.

This book is a map packed with valuable insights into buying a home. The stories come alive as you join Kumar and Kareena on their journey navigating the process of buying their house. It's a book where knowledge, humour and a sprinkle of wisdom are the key ingredients.

All proceeds from the sale of this book will be donated to *The Caribbean Children Foundation*, a charity that pays for children's surgeries in the Caribbean.

Thanks to Anjie, my daughter, who helped me tremendously in bringing this book to fruition.

I am deeply grateful to all the teachers who came to me in different ways and to my clients—I will always remain your humble servant. Packaged in every experience, whether good or bad, is a lesson waiting to be unwrapped.

This book is for homebuyers who want to avoid the same mistakes. Through this story, I hope to guide you toward smart, informed decisions so your dream home doesn't become a financial nightmare.

1 FIRST STEP TOWARDS HOMEOWNERSHIP

Trapped in an elevator with strangers, the couple got their first lesson about buying a home.

Kumar and Kareena had recently immigrated to Canada from India. They wondered how they could have gotten into such a sticky situation in their Toronto apartment building. The elevator had broken down, trapping them and two other residents, Christopher and Louise, in a tiny, sweltering box.

"I'm terrified of elevators and can't wait to leave this building," Louise confessed, trembling.

Christopher held Louise's hand and gently rubbed her back. "Relax and take some deep breaths. Hopefully, we can get out of here soon."

Kareena knew that panicking would only worsen things, even though she was also scared. She handed Louise some tissues.

Louise smiled at Kareena as she patted her eyes with the tissue. "You have a calming personality," she said.

Kumar, a stubby, broad-shouldered individual, looked at Louise. "Kareena meditates a lot, and she's a schoolteacher."

Kumar shook Christopher's hand, and the two began to chat. Kareena stepped over and started talking with Louise. It turned out that Christopher loved Indian cuisine and that Kumar was a gourmet chef. The couple chatted for an hour, forgetting their discomfort, before the elevators started to work again. They exchanged phone numbers and promised to keep in touch.

One day, during dinner with Christopher and Louise, Kumar and Kareena heard that their new friends had recently bought a house and would be moving in months. They were thrilled and eager to learn from their friends' experiences.

After the move, Christopher and Louise invited Kumar and Kareena over for dinner. Over lasagna and salad, they curiously asked about home-buying. They were also determined to buy a home.

"Start by saving. Make a budget and stick to it," advised Christopher. "You can always buy depreciating luxuries later in life."

Christopher and Louise had started saving years before they made their purchase. They bought the maximum RRSP allowed to reduce their income and save on taxes. RRSP, or Registered Retirement Savings Plan, is a tax-advantaged investment account designed to help Canadians save for retirement. When they were ready to buy, they both withdrew RRSP funds to supplement their downpayment, intending to repay the funds within the fifteen-year timeline specified by the Canadian Revenue Agency.

"We have $150,000 saved up so far," declared Kumar.

"That's a good start," Louise said, "but to buy a home, you must put aside about three percent of the purchase price towards acquisition cost. In real estate, they call it a *Closing Costs*, and we can talk about that later. Let's give you a grand tour of our home. As you can see, we don't have much furniture. We concentrated on paying down as much as possible on the house itself."

Christopher and Louise's home was around 1,600 square feet, with two stories and a basement. It had three bedrooms and three and a half bathrooms. Their main bedroom featured a full ensuite.

"Our basement is a basement apartment," said Christopher. "When we bought the home, we met the tenants and decided to continue with them. Keeping it that way has become such a great financial help for us. Lucky for us, this home's basement apartment is already registered with the city."

It was a hot summer day, so Christopher and Kumar went to the backyard with a beer. Meanwhile, Louise and Kareena made themselves comfortable in the air-conditioned living room.

"Our realtor is a great guy," Christopher said as he sipped his beer. "You and Kareena should meet with him. He can walk you through the process if you want. He would know more than us on that topic. His name is Justin. Do you want me to call him?"

Kumar took a swig. "That's a great idea."

Christopher leaned sideways to clink his bottle against Kumar's. "Let's finish this and then join the ladies."

In the living room, Kareena and Louise were drinking iced tea.

"Did you know," Louise said, "that without credit, you cannot establish a credit report, and without a credit report, it's difficult to get a mortgage? Christopher and I have one credit card each. Applying for too many can trigger hard inquiries, which suggest to financial institutions that you're taking on too much debt!"

Kareena nodded. "I know. Maxed-out credit cards would hurt your credit. That's why you should always be mindful."

Louise smiled and agreed. Hearing the backdoor open, they both turned to see Christopher and Kumar entered from the patio, holding their empty bottles.

"Did you guys know we would buy a home earlier, but I had cosigned for a friend's cell phone? She paid her phone bills late, and my credit score dropped!" exclaimed Christopher as he set the empty bottles on the kitchen counter.

Louise nodded somberly. "If you had cosigned for her to buy a home instead of a phone, you would have lost your first-time homebuyer privileges. In the eyes of the lender, we might not have qualified for a mortgage since they could have claimed we were buying a second home." Louise turned to Kareena and waved a finger. "Be careful who and what you cosign for. You need to put yourself first in these situations."

"I learnt my lesson," Christopher said. "Giving someone a dollar is better than co-signing for them."

Louise suddenly sat up, gesturing to Christopher. "Tell them what happened with the lease!" she said before turning to Kareena. "We bought this home with a possession date in September, but we didn't realize we were locked into a lease agreement with our landlord until December!"

"Yep," Christopher said, glancing at Louise. "We got lucky because our landlord managed to find a new tenant, but they took a month's rent as a penalty for breaking the lease." Christopher paused before turning to Kumar. "By the way, you said you had saved $150,000 earlier, right?"

Kumar nodded and looked at Kareena, who had a broad smile. They were both proud that their budgeting efforts had paid off.

"Why don't you invest it to earn some serious cash?" Christopher asked. "Louise and I invested in good dividend stocks."

"Stocks?" repeated Kareena. "I don't know much about those. How about mutual funds?"

Louise shook her head. "That's a long-term thing, and as you know, you can't live in a mutual fund."

Kumar frowned. "Kareena has a student loan of about $15,000, and I have a credit card debt of about $10,000. What should we do?"

"Pay them off," advised Christopher. "Why pay a high interest rate while your savings account earns little? Stop the bleeding."

The couples then discussed the importance of a Tax-Free Saving Account (TFSA).

"Unlike a regular savings account where you make next to nothing, a TFSA is like a fruit basket. Each fruit represents a good stock to invest in. When you sell the stocks, the profit is tax-free," explained Christopher.

Louise nodded. "I learned recently that the TFSA was established in 2009 by the Canadian government to encourage people to save. Since you are opening the account with money you already paid taxes on, when you withdraw, it's tax-free. If you never contributed, your contribution limit grows every year!"

Christopher quickly advised, "Make sure not to go over the contribution limit, and/or use it as a daily trading account, but if you exceed the accumulated limit, the bite from the Canada Revenue Agency (CRA) can be nasty."

The couples were interrupted by a beeping from the stove.

"Oh!" exclaimed Louise. "The food's done! Let's put this talk away for now and enjoy dinner! We invited you over to eat, not overwhelm you with information!"

When Kumar and Kareena headed toward their car, it was dark. Christopher and Louise saw them off, standing by their front door with arms around each other.

Louise gasped, leaning forward to shout before Kumar and Kareena could enter their car. "Before I forget, you guys will have to take a stress test before you can get approved for a mortgage!"

Kareena waved in acknowledgement, filing that information away with everything else she and Kumar had learned tonight. "Honey, that stress test reminded me of something. We need to make an appointment to meet Dr. Saied soon," she murmured.

Kumar nodded and started the car. "Yes, you're right. The stress test is important. Let's make the call tomorrow."

For now, they would go home and reflect on everything they had learned. Christopher and Louise had been a wealth of information.

Over dinner that night, Kumar and Kareena made a list of what they learned from their first house-hunting venture today...

LESSONS LEARNED

● **Create and stick to a budget—focus on necessities and avoid non-urgent expenses.**

● **Decide on the house size, considering future family plans.**

● **A city-approved basement apartment can provide extra income for the mortgage.**

● **Build credit wisely—limit credit cards and use them only for necessities.**

● **Never co-sign for someone—it affects your credit rating.**

● **Time our house purchase to align with your lease ending to avoid extra costs.**

● **Pay off outstanding loans faster.**

● **Research the Stress Test—it's important (and stressful!).**

2 LEARNING REAL ESTATE LINGO

From stress tests to home equity, buying a home is more than saving for a downpayment—it's about knowing the lingo.

"*B*ad news, Kareena. Your blood pressure is high!" said Dr. Saied, their family physician. He looked at Kareena and asked, "What made your blood pressure climb?"

Kumar and Kareena had thought that buying a home would be easy. Kareena thought back to the conversation they had a few nights ago with Christopher and Louise. "My friend said that Kumar and I needed a stress test to buy a house. I think I'm all stressed out about that. Why is that a thing?" she burst out.

"I see you came prepared, running shoes and all," intoned Dr. Saied. "Lenders require buyers to have a *financial* stress test, not one for their health. A financial stress test calculates how much a buyer can afford and, if the interest rate increases, whether they can afford a heavier financial burden. It has nothing to do with your heart. My dad is a realtor, and growing up, I learned many things from him."

Kareena pulled out her notebook and pen from her bag.

"Like what?" asked Kumar.

"My dad dealt with a client named Patrick years ago who wanted to borrow money. My dad had explained that he could only lend Patrick money if the home had enough equity."

"Equity?" repeated Kareena, her pen poised over her notebook.

"Yes. Equity is the chunk of money remaining after deducting the amount owed on the mortgage from the current sale price of the home. It's how much *skin* Patrick had in the game," explained Dr. Saeid. "Based on the interest rate and the length of the mortgage, a portion of your payment goes towards the interest, and the remainder to reduce the principal. My dad lent Patrick money as a second mortgage—a mortgage taken out on a home with a first mortgage. If Patrick couldn't pay the mortgages, the first lender or mortgagee could sell the property, and if there was any money left over, then my dad would get paid. My dad said it was risky, but the higher the risk, the higher the reward. Interest rates on second mortgages are much higher than first mortgages so that you can recover your loan faster."

"More skin, less risk. I understand," responded Kumar, "but how did you know how much equity Patrick had in his home?"

"He needed an appraisal on his property," Dr. Saeid answered. "An appraisal is a recent estimate of the value of the property. A licensed property appraiser would research the property through the multiple listing service, MLS."

"What is that?" asked Kareena.

"It's a real estate service that collects data on properties for sale and those that all the realtors sold, who are members," replied Dr. Saeid.

Kareena fumbled in her purse and extracted a page about a property. "Dr. Saied, this paper mentioned that the home comes with ELFs, GDO and BDLM. I know what elves are, but what are the others?"

Dr. Saied laughed. "This piece of paper is called a listing. ELFs are the short form for *Electrical Light Fixtures*, GDO is for *Garage Door Openers*, CAC is for *Central Air conditioning*, and BDLM means *Broadloom Where Laid*."

"Oh!" laughed Kareena. "Not elves! I was so confused!" She scribbled notes in her book.

Dr. Saied laughed with the couple. "By the way," he asked, recalling his dad's experiences with past buyers. "Have you gotten pre-qualified for a mortgage yet?"

"As a teacher, I thought you only qualify after passing an exam. Are you telling me I'm pre-qualified before passing my exam?" Kareena joked.

"You know, Dr. Saied," Kumar chimed in. "I heard there was a difference between being *pre-qualified* and *pre-approved*, but I can't make heads or tails of it!"

"Pre-qualified in real estate means that the lender looks at your financial history and gives you an estimate of how much money they are willing to lend you," Dr. Saeid explained. "Pre-approval, on the other hand, imposes responsibilities—it's where the buyer completes an application and all the necessary documentation for review and the lender firms up on how much to lend you."

"Looks like we have to get pre-qualified, then qualified," snickered Kareena. "Postmortem, mortuary and mortgage. It seems as if having a mortgage is a death sentence."

"The word *mort* means death, and *gage* connotes a pledge." Dr. Saeid sounded as if he were lecturing. "A mortgage is a security, usually the property, given for a loan and must be paid back even if the borrower dies. The lender is the mortgagee and the borrower the mortgagor."

"I saw a listing that said it's an assignment sale. What is that?" said Kumar.

Dr. Saeid thought momentarily, trying to recall the knowledge his father had shared over the years. "An assignment sale is when a buyer of a property signs over the rights and obligations to that property before the official closing. Some people call it flipping."

"Hamburgers and houses—you can flip them both," joked Kareena. "When the grill is hot, flipping happens more often."

"That about sounds right," Dr. Saied said.

"Thanks, Dr. Saied, for your help as a doctor and for sharing this knowledge. You're a kind man doing lots of good deeds," acknowledged Kumar.

"You know," Kareena piped up. "I heard that when we buy a home, the home must also have good deeds."

"Yes, that's true," said Dr. Saied, nodding slowly. "A house deed transfers ownership from the seller to the buyer in real estate. When you have a mortgage, you have a transfer deed because the lender has the deed for the property as security for the money they lent."

"I guess we will only have some easement from our troubles after buying our home," commented Kumar.

Dr Saied's lips trembled with a smile. "An easement gives someone else the legal right to use another person's property. You have easements for utility companies. It can also be a right of way to access another landlocked property," he clarified.

"Do you mean that person has the right to enter our property, and we can do nothing about it?" Kareena said.

"That about sums it up," Dr. Saied said.

"Does it also mean they can change our property without our consent?"

"No, it doesn't. It just gives a third party the right to access your property, such as fixing a Hydro or Gas line that might have a problem. Or to make repairs to their property."

"We spent a lot of time with you today." Kumar sat up. "Simply speaking, how much is your fee?"

"There is no fee today; it's all covered by OHIP, but in real estate, there is something called *fee-simple*," Dr. Saied said, eyes now twinkling with amusement. He was having a lot of fun with the wordplay in their conversation. "I'll give you one last real estate tidbit. Did you know that fee-simple is when the owner's rights to the property are absolute and can only be transferred whenever the owner chooses? It's the most common type of ownership. Most often, it's associated with freehold properties. Condominiums are usually bought with certain restrictions and are not considered *fee-simple*."

Kumar and Kareena finally left at twilight. They had spent much longer than expected at Dr. Saeid's office but had learned a lot. As they reflected on the information they had uncovered, it was a quiet drive home.

"We are lucky to have Dr. Saied as our family doctor, and even luckier, we were his last patients. His dad taught him well. I guess the stars are aligning, Kareena."

"Yes," Kareena agreed with a smile. She reached out to grasp Kumar's hand and squeezed it. "They certainly are. Let's start looking for our dream home." She waved her notebook at him. "But right after dinner, we should review what we learnt today."

LESSONS LEARNED

- **Equity = Current market value - Outstanding principal.**

- **Paying more and faster on the principal increases equity.**

- **Stress Test (Canada): Determines mortgage eligibility based on regulations.**

- **MLS (Multiple Listing Service): Platform for property listings and values.**

- **Pre-qualification vs. Pre-approval:**

  - **Pre-qualified: Estimate of loan amount.**

- ○ **Pre-approved: Requires application for a firm mortgage amount.**

- **Easements: Except for utilities, they can cause issues, so avoid properties with them.**

- **Transfer Deed: Essential document for ownership.**

3 KUMAR AND KAREENA'S UNEXPECTED TEACHER

Valuable insights about REITs, investment strategies, and the power of experience.

Saturday nights at the banquet hall were always hectic for Kumar, the main chef. After finishing his night shift, Kumar finally arrived home at 2:00 a.m.

On Sunday morning, he sank into bed, careful not to disturb Kareena but eager to catch up on his sleep. Today would be his day to relax.

As 9:00 a.m. approached, Kareena's phone rang. She woke up suddenly, groggily glancing at her phone on the nightstand. Kumar slept soundly beside her, and she didn't want to wake him. Reaching to turn it off, she noticed the name on the screen: Dr. Saied was calling. Kareena's heart began to race as she picked up the phone.

"Dr. Saied?" Kareena asked in a whisper, moving to get out of bed.

"Good morning, Kareena!" Dr. Saeid greeted her with a cheerful tone. "I'm off to the seniors' home to volunteer today. I'm just checking if you and Kumar would like to join me."

"We wouldn't mind," Kareena whispered, "but Kumar is still asleep."

"I'll be here from two to five p.m."

Once Kumar woke up and Kareena updated him on the doctor's phone call, the two enjoyed a peaceful morning before heading to the neighbourhood's seniors' home. When they arrived, they asked about the doctor's location. The receptionist directed them to one of the residents' rooms.

"Kareena! Kumar!" Dr. Saeid called out to them as he knelt before an older woman, cleaning and trimming her nails. "Allow me to introduce you to Mila!" he said, rising to his feet. "Mila immigrated from Texas in her mid-twenties. She worked for a real estate conglomerate for thirty-five years before retiring. She has a wealth of information!"

Mila greeted the couple with a warm smile. "Dr. Saeid mentioned that a young couple would be stopping by and were interested in real estate. If you have the time, I'd love to share some of what I've learned over the years."

Kumar and Kareena smiled and sat on the small couch opposite Mila's bed.

"We would love that, Mila," Kareena said. "Kumar and I want to buy a house, but we have no idea where to begin. Any advice would be appreciated!"

"Well," Mila said, nudging Dr. Saied playfully. "Over the years, I've built tremendous wealth through my company. One thing I always advise is to invest in REITs. Every young person should consider this to grow their wealth. If you're renting and saving for a down payment on a home, you can invest in liquid real estate."

Kumar frowned. "REITs? I don't know if I've ever heard of that."

Dr. Saied smiled and continued cleaning Mila's feet as she got more comfortable. "Mila is an expert in this. While I know some stuff about real estate because of my dad, Mila was in the game."

Mila dipped her feet in the warm bowl of water. "REIT stands for *Real Estate Investment Trust.* Liquid real estate refers to partial ownership of properties that you can quickly convert into cash. Selling a property is complex and can take a long time to close, but REITs can be bought and sold like stocks. A REIT is an investment company that buys, manages, or finances income-producing real estate, such as shopping centres, medical buildings, and apartment buildings," Mila recited diligently.

Dr. Saied smiled at Kareena and Kumar. "This is one of the best places to volunteer. The people here are full of life lessons and wisdom. I learn something new every time I visit."

Kareena sat forward, thinking for a moment. "So, is a REIT like a well-managed rental property?" she asked hesitantly.

"Yes," Mila confirmed, "but on a grander scale. You can own units in luxury apartment buildings or major shopping centres. The idea is to pool money from different investors and then use that capital to buy or finance real estate."

Dr. Saied nodded. "I remember my dad saying REITs are specialized. Is that true, Mila?"

Mila patted Dr. Saeid's shoulder. "You remember well, doctor! Some REITs may focus on owning and managing medical buildings, while others opt to acquire rundown properties, modernize them, and charge higher rent. Canadian REITs are generally a safe, low-risk investment with a clear agenda. While purchasing an investment property requires a hefty down payment, a unit share in a REIT is relatively inexpensive."

Kareena rummaged in her purse and pulled out her notepad and pen. "I don't want to forget this!"

Mila beamed, eager to share her knowledge. She rarely had the chance to discuss her previous job, and she wouldn't waste this opportunity. "Some REITs maintain a mixed portfolio of properties, which offers stability for the company because if one sector of the economy is down, the other sector might perform well. The trust will collect rental income, pay all expenses, and then distribute the profits to the unit holders."

"How much is the profit?" Kumar interjected.

"Great question!" Mila replied, unfazed by the interruption. "Typically, it's between 85% and 95%. REITs benefit from not being taxed at the trust level, allowing more income to reach the unit holders and be considered regular income. Including REITs in a TFSA is an excellent tax-saving strategy. However, as you might know, a TFSA is tax-free when you withdraw funds, as contributions come from after-tax income."

Dr Saied washed Mila's feet and dried them with a soft towel. "What do you suggest you look for if you want to invest in REITs, Mila?"

Mila took a moment to think. "Look for reputable companies and their current portfolios. I would choose REITs based on which real estate market segment is about to boom. For instance, as baby boomers age, health care has immense potential. Companies that invest in medical buildings, retirement homes, and outpatient care are likely to outperform in the long run. There are three fundamental metrics to consider when buying REITs. The first is the cap rate."

"I've read about that!" Kumar exclaimed, excited to share what he'd learned. "Cap rate reflects the rate of return on the investment. To calculate the cap rate, divide the net operating income by the current market value."

"Yes," confirmed Mila. "Cap rates above six percent are decent, considering the current interest rate. Have you heard of funds from operations?"

Kumar shook his head. "Never have," he confirmed.

"Funds From Operations, or FFO, represent the actual cash flow from the REIT. You can calculate it by taking the net income from all sources and adding non-cash flow items such as depreciation expenses and any non-operating gains or losses, like those incurred in the sale of assets. What about *Adjusted Funds From Operations*?"

"I know that one!" Dr. Saeid exclaimed. "It's also referred to as AFFO. You can calculate Adjusted funds from operations by making specific adjustments to the FFO. When determining the FFO, consider the average cost of maintaining and repairing the property. With the AFFO, you factor in the actual expenses. My dad used to say that AFFO is a better indicator of REIT's performance."

"That's completely right!" Mila said, impressed with Dr. Saeid's knowledge. "You have a good memory, doctor."

"Not as good as yours," Dr. Saeid countered. "You're sharp as a whip."

"You should have seen me when I was thirty; I was sharper!" Mila laughed, enjoying the company.

"How do you all feel about everything so far?"

"I think I'm following," Kumar said, hesitantly.

They were interrupted by a knock on the door. Kareena opened the door to find one of the workers wheeling a serving table with refreshments.

"It's teatime, Mila." The worker said, greeting Mila with a friendly smile.

The worker gave Mila tea and snacks before proceeding to the other rooms. Kareena took a bite of her cookie, reflecting on everything discussed.

"Mila," Kareena asked as she reviewed her notes. "You've mentioned a lot about REITs, but are there any drawbacks?"

Mila nodded, taking a sip of her tea. "That's an excellent question. Like most things in life, there always are. High management fees can erode profitability. An increase in interest rates can trigger higher borrowing costs and, consequently, a lower yield. Since publicly traded REITs must pay out almost ninety percent of their profits, REITs generally experience weaker growth. A unit holder does not have control over day-to-day operations compared to direct investment."

"How about those mortgages where people pool money together and then lend it out?" asked Dr. Saied.

Mila wagged a finger at him. "Don't confuse a REIT with syndicated mortgages," she scolded playfully. "Syndicated mortgages allow small investors to pool their money together for a large-scale development with the promise of a healthy return. Syndicated mortgages are extremely high risk."

Dr. Saied smiled at Mila. He gathered up the dishes and patted Mila's shoulder. "It's been a pleasure, as always. I've got some other patients to see, and you must get dressed for dinner. Cocktail hour is at six this afternoon."

Mila laughed. "That reminds me," she said, winking at Kareena. "REITs make a fantastic addition when mixed with other real estate investments. They allow investors to enjoy real estate ownership benefits without worries. However, traditional real estate consistently outperforms in the long run."

"Is there anything else you'd recommend?" Kumar asked as he stood, eager to absorb as much information as possible before they departed.

Mila nodded. "I would consider allocating ten percent of my portfolio to REITs and investing the remainder in rental properties. This would serve as a safety net to access cash quickly if necessary. REITs are outstanding wealth builders for long-term savings, such as in an RRSP or TFSA account."

"Thank you for sharing so much knowledge," Dr Saied said as he headed out.

"Yes," agreed Kareena, bending to hug Mila.

"Anytime!" Mila exclaimed with a cheerful smile. "This was a lovely visit. You can visit me anytime, with or without the good doctor."

Kumar smiled. "We may just take you up on that, ma'am."

The trio left Mila's room, and Dr. Saeid escorted Kumar and Kareena to the door. "I have more residents to see, but thank you for accepting my invitation, even if it was last minute. I remembered our conversation about real estate and thought this would be a wonderful learning opportunity for both of you."

"It was," Kumar said, extending his hand to shake Dr. Saied's. "Thank you for considering us, doctor. I learned much from Mila and will revisit her!"

"Yes," agreed Kareena. "Thank you for reaching out to us. I always thought you were wise beyond your age. Now we know why."

Dr. Saied clapped them both on the shoulder. "I learned a saying from one of the residents here: *I hear, and I forget. I see, and I remember. I do, and I understand.*"

"Excellent advice," Kumar said, nudging Kareena.

Kareena returned the smile. "How should we spend the rest of your day off?" she asked Kumar as they headed to the car.

"Let's relax for now," Kumar decided. "But next Sunday, let's come back. I have a great cookie recipe, and I'm sure Mila would enjoy them. To put it in Dr. Saied's words: *That sums it up*! It's still overwhelming, though, and I'm glad you're taking notes for us to review as we go along."

Kareena said, "Remember his parting words: *I hear and forget. I see, and I remember. I do, and I understand*! But let's sit in the car and review the lessons learned from today's visit," she said.

LESSONS LEARNED

- **REIT means Real Estate Investment Trust. Here in Canada, it's a convenient way of creating a diversified real estate portfolio without buying a property.**
- **The central portion of a REIT's profit is returned to shareholders, who pay the tax. The net proceeds can be invested in an RRSP or if the investment is held in a TFSA, it's tax-free when you withdraw it.**
- **Cap Rate stands for *Capitalization Rate*. We arrive at it by dividing the Net Operating Income by the Current Market Value of the property we are considering. It's the rate of return the REIT provides for shareholders. When comparing property rates, we should look at rates that are six percent higher or above.**
- **FFO stands for *Funds From Operations* and represents the actual cash flow from the REIT. This affects the payout to shareholders, so the higher the payout, the better.**
- **AFFO stands for *Adjusted Funds From Operations*. It is calculated by taking the Net Operating Income in the FFO and subtracting non-cash flow items, such as depreciation and non-operating gains from asset sales. Likewise, you would add back non-operating losses. This adjustment allows you to focus on income that can be distributed to shareholders continuously,**

making **AFFO** a superior measure for comparing the performance of REITs.
- Oh, and they also discussed *Syndicated Mortgages*. These are when investors pool their money to lend on projects like large-scale developments. While the return can be high, the risk is also high.

4 BIRTHDAY SURPRISE & FINANCIAL INSPIRATION

Kareena's 25th birthday celebration takes a twist—the couple discovers the power of a First Home Savings Account.

Kareena's twenty-fifth birthday was last Saturday. Kumar and Kareena's friends and relatives surprised her with a party at Kareena's parents' home. Kumar prepared most of the food at the banquet hall. Noha and Emma, two of Kareena's school friends, also came.

Kareena was emotional. "This is indeed a surprise! I am fortunate to have so many loving family and friends here."

Emma gave Kareena a tight hug. "Congratulations on your twenty-fifth. Noha and I got here just in time. Today, we attended a homebuyer workshop and learned about the *First Home Savings Account*."

Kareena quickly reached into her purse, took out her notebook and pen, and signaled Kumar to join them. "Kumar and I are planning on buying our first home. We are not aware of the First Home Savings Account."

Noha smiled. "The First Home Savings Account (FHSA) offers first-time home buyers a powerful tool to save for their dream home with unique tax benefits."

Emma squeezed Kareena's hand gently. "Do you know that the FHSA allows first-time home buyers to contribute up to $8,000 annually, with a lifetime cap of $40,000?"

Noha scratched his head gently. "When you buy a FHSA, it reduces your taxable income, like an RRSP."

Kumar asked, " Do we have to pay tax when we withdraw the money to buy our first home?"

"Withdrawals for a down payment are tax-free, like a TFSA," answered Noha.

Emma unconsciously went into teaching mode. "To qualify, you must not currently own a home. If your spouse owns your principal residence, you cannot open an FHSA, as the house is considered a matrimonial property."

"This is interesting," said Kareena. "Let's have some Indian dessert Kumar made."

As they approached the dining table, Noha explained that opening an FHSA can save you money by allowing you to pay less tax. "If you're in a higher tax bracket, contributing before year-end maximizes your refund. Contributions made during the calendar year qualify for that year's tax deduction.

"You can carry forward unused contribution room up to $8,000 to the following year. Even if you're unsure about buying soon, an FHSA grows tax-free, and you can transfer any extra funds to your RRSP without impacting your RRSP contribution limit."

"Indian sweets are yummy, but I must be careful. What is sweet on the lips shows up in the hips," commented Emma.

Kareena burst out laughing. "You don't have to worry, Emma; you look like a sweet sixteen."

Noha said, "Yes, Emma, you have a lot of room. Besides, you will burn out at the gym. Can we open a joint FHSA?"

"Opening a separate FHSA is better because it doubles your savings potential. You can contribute toward buying a home, even if only one of you is on the mortgage," said Emma. "If you plan on buying a house under two years, one option is in low-risk options like GICs. For the long term, an option is ETFs in Canadian bank stocks but it's important to seek help from a financial advisor before making decisions like this."

Kumar took a deep, slow breath. "We had a financial adviser before and concluded that no one can care for our money better than ourselves. The banks make billions in profit and pay good dividends, and that's a safe bet."

Noha took a sip of his gin. "With an FHSA, you must use the funds to buy your principal residence and not an investment property, and you must close the account by the end of the year you buy your home. CRA requires you to live in the home within one year of purchase."

Justin, Kumar's and Kareena's realtor, and Bibi, their mortgage broker, joined the conversation.

"You can transfer funds from your RRSP into your FHSA. This strategy is beneficial if you have little RRSP room or large pensions," said Bibi. "Under the Home Buyer's Plan, you can increase your downpayment by combining your FHSA and RRSP withdrawals."

Kareena pulled up a chair and flopped down. "Opening an FHSA is a smart idea, but what happens if I have extra money after buying a home?"

"You can convert it into an RRSP," said Emma.

Justin put his plate down. "Opening an FHSA is an excellent idea because you can save on taxes and grow your portfolio without paying taxes."

Kumar stroked his beard. "What do we need to know to open an FHSA?"

Emma had the answer. "You must be a Canadian resident between eighteen and seventy-one."

"To open an account, you'll need your SIN, date of birth, and supporting documents." Emma also explained that it's advisable to add a beneficiary.

It was almost midnight, and the birthday girl began to yawn.

Kareena closed her notebook and looked at Kumar. "Landlords grow rich in their sleep. We need to stop paying rent and invest in a home."

The following day, Kareena reviewed her notes about FHSA with Kumar.

LESSONS LEARNED

- First-time buyers between the ages of 18 and 71 can open an FHSA.

- We can open separate FHSAs.

- We can contribute $8,000 yearly, to a maximum of $40,000.

- For the long term, we can invest in good dividend stocks.

- If we plan on buying within two years, let's opt for a short term investment.

- FHSAs have a dual benefit. They work like RRSPs and TFSAs. We can save on taxes and grow the money tax-free.

- After we buy our home, we can convert the extra to an RRSP.

5 BUYER REPRESENTATION AGREEMENTS

Pricey mistakes and the impact of choosing the right realtor.

Friday nights were social occasions for Kumar and Kareena. They had invited their friend Sebastian and his girlfriend, Lizzy, to drop by. With Kumar being a chef, a feast awaited them upon their arrival.

They took some time to catch up and soon enjoyed the ambiance, having not seen each other for a while.

"We went to see our realtor today," Kareena remarked as they ate. "His name is Justin. He provided us with a buyer's contract to review. We will meet with him next week to discuss it."

Sebastian quickly put his wine glass down, shaking his head. "Don't sign that—those can be death traps!"

"A drunken lip reveals a sober mind," Lizzy remarked. "Sebastian had a negative experience with one of those."

Sebastian took a long sip of his wine. "Two years ago, when I bought my home, I worked with a realtor for two months before making an offer on a property I liked," he said slowly. "There was a lot of paperwork to sign. My realtor said it was standard when purchasing a home. I lost the property because the seller and I disagreed with the price. I told my realtor I didn't want to work with him any longer. The next thing I knew, I received an invoice from his office for $17,495.50, with $8,150.00 due upon receipt!"

"What?" exclaimed Kareena in disbelief. "Why did you have to pay him any money?"

"I signed a *Buyer Agency Agreement* with this realtor for one year without realizing it. It was one of those forms among all the paperwork my realtor had me sign. I had to consult a lawyer, and that's how I met Lizzy."

Lizzy smiled at them. "I'm a legal secretary at the litigation law firm that Seb approached. Some realtors represent the seller even when they are acting for the buyer. If you share confidential information with your realtor as a buyer, he can tell the seller in these situations. However, if you sign a Buyer Representation Agreement, your realtor is legally required to protect your interests. Your realtor cannot disclose any information to the other party that might undermine your negotiating power."

"That's referred to as fiduciary duties," Kumar and Kareena said simultaneously. They had been studying real estate recently.

Lizzy nodded. "I once handled a case where a buyer signed a *Buyer Agency Agreement* for three months. She was unaware she had done so, as it was part of the paperwork. Unhappy with her realtor, she soon purchased a home with another realtor."

"I remember you telling me this," commented Sebastian.

"After the deal closed," Lizzy continued, "the first realtor sued the buyer for commission plus interest and legal fees."

"Buying a home is the biggest purchase most people make in a lifetime," Sebastian commented.

Lizzy nodded. "*Buyer Representation Agreements* are designed to protect buyers. However, it's essential to read what you're signing and remember that once you sign a document, you should keep a copy for your records."

Lizzy and Sebastian assisted Kumar and Kareena with the cleanup before they departed. Kumar and Kareena chose to linger outside a bit longer, savoring the fresh air before bedtime.

"Honey," Kareena said, gently shaking Kumar before he could doze off in the lawn chair. "I'm happy we found Justin. Some realtors would have had us sign the paperwork without even reviewing it."

"Christopher and Louise referred him," Kumar said sleepily. "You're right, though. Not everyone would take the time to explain the forms we have to sign. I guess that's why choosing a professional is important."

"That reminds me. We need to make an appointment soon. Let's call him in the morning."

Kumar nodded. They were ready for the next step.

"Don't fall asleep on me before we review the lessons learned today," Kareena said.

LESSONS LEARNED

- **Get Advice First:** Never sign documents with a realtor without fully understanding the conditions.

- **Buyer Representation Agreement:** This agreement ensures that the agent works only for us and doesn't share information with the seller's agent.

- **Keep Copies Safe:** Store agreements securely for easy access when needed.

6 UNDERSTANDING BUYER CONTRACTS

How a conversation with a realtor changed Kumar and Kareena's viewpoint on homeownership.

As a chef, Kumar was often busy in the evenings. Tonight, he was catering to 300 guests at the banquet hall. Although he had made most of the preparations beforehand, he had much to do this evening.

As he kissed Kareena goodbye, his thoughts drifted from the enormous workload awaiting him at the banquet hall to whether he and Kareena should postpone buying a home until they could save more money.

Once Kumar arrived at the banquet hall, he noticed the support staff was already there. In a few hours, the guests would come, and everything had to be flawlessly synchronized. Fortunately, it was a well-established routine for the workers.

After a partaking in a sumptuous meal, the guests took to the dance floor. Kumar left early, eager to share his thoughts with Kareena. When he arrived, she was getting ready for bed.

"I'm having second thoughts about buying a home right now," Kumar admitted as he joined Kareena. "Maybe we should wait and save more money to increase our down payment."

Kareena paused and then weighed her words carefully. "The way I see it, by the time we manage to save another $20,000 to $30,000, the price of homes might have already increased. And if the price rises higher than the amount we can save, we may be in a worse position. I believe this is a decision we should not take lightly. Let's set up a meeting with Justin. Perhaps he can guide us through the process before we decide."

Kumar beamed. "I appreciated how he explained everything thoroughly and addressed all our questions."

"He has a good reputation in real estate."

The following day, Kumar and Kareena met Justin at his office.

"I want to congratulate you on taking a giant leap toward homeownership. It's a long and cumbersome process, and as you know, the journey of a thousand miles begins with the first step," Justin said with a pleasant smile, shaking their hand.

Kumar turned to Justin. "You're right about the journey, but we could easily get lost without a proper guide. Could you please provide us with some directions?"

Justin smiled with confidence. "Before I can advise, tell me what's on your mind."

"The other day," Kareena began, "we were talking to some friends, and one of them told me never to sign a *Buyer's Representation Agreement*."

"Yes!" Kumar added, remembering Sebastian's insistence on signing the form. "Our friend mentioned that he had a negative experience with one of those!"

Justin nodded. "Yes, a realtor might ask you to sign a Buyer Representation Agreement when buying a home. This agreement defines the nature of the relationship between you and the brokerage," he explained. "I'm sorry your friend had a bad experience; this is why choosing a realtor is crucial. Realtors must act fairly, honestly, and with integrity, providing conscientious service to you—the clients. If you have any reservations about the form, I can explain it in detail."

"That would be helpful," Kareena admitted, glancing at Kumar. "We trust you, Justin, but we also want to know what we will sign."

"Absolutely," Justin said with a smile. "Both of you are doing the right thing by asking for explanations. You shouldn't sign documents you don't understand. A Buyer's Representation Agreement has four important aspects to review. The first is that it includes a time commitment."

"What time commitment? How long will it take us to find a house?" asked Kumar.

"Not exactly," explained Justin. "The agreement specifies that you will work with only one brokerage— the one I represent—during that time frame. You can determine the duration of the agreement by mutual consent between you and the brokerage. You must acknowledge this if it exceeds six months by initialing here." Justin pointed to the relevant spot on the agreement he was clarifying.

"What's the second thing?" Kareena asked as she took out her notebook and pen.

"Location," Justin replied. You can tailor a *Buyer Agreement* to a specific area, such as Toronto or the Peel Region, or it can cover the entire province of Ontario, a neighbourhood, or even a particular home. This distinction is crucial because you won't be locked into an agreement if you move to a different area and wish to collaborate with a local realtor."

"So, if we've signed a Buyer's Agreement with a realtor for a location in Toronto, can we sign another one with a realtor in Barrie?" Kumar asked, trying to make sense of the situation.

"As long as the agreement specifies the location," Justin added. "The agreement outlines the relationship between you and the brokerage. Now, the third thing to be aware of is the *Holdover Clause*. Have either of you heard of this before?"

Kumar and Kareena shook their heads.

"What this means," Justin explained, "is that if you terminate your relationship with a brokerage but then buy a property that was presented to you while the Buyer Agency Agreement was active, you will owe a commission to the brokerage for a specified period. Always negotiate the holdover period before signing the agreement."

"That's fairly straightforward," Kareena said to Kumar.

"Finally," Justin said, "let's discuss the commission rate. Keep in mind that there are no fixed fees for purchasing a home. Brokerages may offer various percentages for commission rates based on their business practices. My brokerage, for example, usually requests two and a half percent of the purchase price. In most instances, the seller pays this commission; however, in private sales where the seller does not cover this cost, you would be responsible for paying for my brokerage's services."

Kumar took a deep breath. "It's challenging to navigate purchasing a home without genuine guidance."

Justin nodded. "That's why I like to say a good realtor is like an experienced sea captain. You need someone reliable to navigate stormy waters."

"Is that all, Justin?" Kareena asked after finishing her review of the *Buyer's Agreement*. "There's a lot of fine print here, so I appreciate you providing details."

"There's one more thing I'd like to expand on before we proceed," Justin said. "It's called multiple representation, which occurs when a brokerage represents both the buyer and the seller. There might be times when two buyers, working with the same realtor, want to buy the same home, which is also multiple representation. If that happens, I must obtain written consent confirming that both parties understand this."

"That's fair," said Kareena. "After all, it must be a win-win for everyone."

"It's not just a win-win," Justin said, "but we strive to be fair to all parties involved. Multiple representation doesn't happen very often, but I prefer to be upfront about any potential situations that may arise. If you decide to make an offer on a property where I also represent the seller or another buyer, that would involve multiple representations."

"That makes sense," Kumar said. "Thank you for taking the time to explain the contract to us."

Kareena nodded. "We've spoken with a few other realtors, but none provided as much detail as you have. We truly appreciate that." She exchanged a knowing glance with Kumar and clapped her hands. "Let's get the process underway! Where would you like us to sign?"

That night, around the dinner table, Kareena pulled out her notebook and reviewed the points they had discussed with Justin that day.

LESSONS LEARNED

- We needed an honest and upfront agent—Justin fits the bill.
- We do not sign any documents until:
  - All clauses are clarified.
  - We did our research.
  - We can ask a lawyer to review the papers if necessary.
- The safe sign-up period is 60 days, with an extension only if we are satisfied with the agent.
- We have decided to stay in Peel Region, so this should be included in the Buyer Agreement.
- We should avoid getting into Multiple representations (when a broker represents both buyer and seller).

7 CRUNCHING THE SLICES

From mortgage math to pizza, Bibi prepares a financial roadmap for the couple.

Summer days were lovely, especially this Tuesday morning, and Kumar took the day off. Kareena was enjoying her summer break.

"I collected twigs and built toy houses when I was five," Kumar joked. They lounged on the apartment balcony, enjoying the warm weather and summer breeze. "Guruji told me that if I wanted something badly, I had to sit and focus on what I wanted and experience the process as if I had already achieved it."

"I've been doing that!" exclaimed Kareena. "When I meditate, I can envision our new home!"

Later that afternoon, the two went to see Bibi, a mortgage broker Justin had referred them to. When they arrived, Bibi welcomed them both with a warm smile.

"Congratulations!" she exclaimed, shaking Kumar and Kareena's hand. "Justin explained the situation to me. You two are on the right track to buying your home!"

"Thanks," Kumar replied before sitting in Bibi's office and motioning for Kareena to join him. "We have no idea how any of this works."

"That's where valued professionals like Justin and I come in," Bibi replied. She sat down across from them. "So, do you like pizza?"

Kumar and Kareena shared a puzzled glance.

"Pizza?" Kareena echoed. "I adore pizza, especially when it has extra toppings!"

"What does pizza have to do with our financing?" Kumar asked, still confused.

Bibi smiled. "Think of your total gross income as a giant pizza," she explained. "Let's cut it into three slices. The first slice is approximately one-third or 32%, the second is 10%, and the last is 58%."

"Who gets the biggest slice?" Kumar asked.

"You keep the largest slice," Bibi emphasized. "The other 32% covers your mortgage and property tax, while the remaining 10% is for your current debts."

"That makes sense to me," Kareena affirmed.

"Good," Bibi replied. "So, approximately how much is your combined income?"

Kumar paused for a moment. "About $150,000," he replied, and Kareena nodded.

"Well done!" Bibi exclaimed. Your combined income is $150,000, which is excellent. If we take 32% of that, your gross debt ratio (GDR) will be around $48,000. Lenders will allow you an additional 10% to cover other debts, such as credit cards and student loans."

"We're paying $500 monthly on our car loan," Kareena said, and Bibi jotted down the information.

"Don't forget the $300 for student loans and another $200 for miscellaneous," added Kumar.

"Alright," said Bibi, quickly doing the math. "That works out to be $1,000 monthly or $12,000 yearly. Based on your combined income of $150,000, 10% is around $15,000. Congratulations that means you're within our qualifying guidelines!"

Kumar and Kareena exchanged a high-five with a grin.

"We're a step ahead of the game!" Kumar exclaimed in excitement.

"Certainly," Bibi agreed. "Now, remember the two small slices? Those make up 42% of your pizza. That's called your Total Debt Service, or TDS. Lenders can use their discretion based on your credit and spending habits to increase the ratio slightly."

"So you have Gross Debt Service and Total Debt Service?" Kareena said.

"Yes," Bibi confirmed. "Your GDS is $48,000 divided by twelve since there are twelve months in a year. That's $4,000 monthly. Let's assume that property tax is around $400 monthly, meaning you can afford a mortgage payment of $3,600 monthly."

"That's good to know!" exclaimed Kumar.

"Let's see how much mortgage we can get based on a monthly payment of $3,600," Bibi said, nodding. "Just be knowledgeable that the stress test rules apply."

Kareena looked at Kumar. "We know what a stress test is in real estate!" she declared.

"That's amazing!" Bibi said in acknowledgement. "The stress test qualifying rate is around 2% higher than the regular mortgage rate. With the stress test, buyers lose about 20% of their purchasing ability."

"That's a lot!" acknowledged Kumar.

"Yes, but the banks want to know that if there is a rate increase, you can carry the mortgage," Bibi responded. "Let's assume that the qualifying rate is 6% — then, for every $1,000 you borrow, you would need to make a monthly payment of $6.44. Are you both still with me?"

Kumar and Kareena nodded.

"It's a lot of math," said Kareena, "but I'm following. If we divide $3,600 by $6.44 and gross up the figure, that equals around $560,000."

"Yes," confirmed Bibi. "Adding your down payment of around $150,000 means you cannot exceed a purchase price of $710,000. Since your down payment is around 20%, you do not need to pay CMHC fees."

"What is CMHC?" Kumar said.

"CMHC stands for Canada Mortgage and Housing Corporation," explained Bibi. "It's a federal crown corporation responsible for assisting with affordable housing in Canada through housing programs like the first-time home buyer loan. It also acts as an insurer for high-leverage loans. Let's pretend you're the lender, and I want to buy a home for $600,000, but I only have $30,000 to put down. You say you can lend me $570,000. Between you and me, who is at a higher risk?"

"The lender is," Kareena confidently answered.

"They have much more skin in the game," Kumar said.

"Yes, they do," agreed Bibi. "By the time a buyer has saved up enough money to offset the lender's risk, home prices will have kept on climbing."

"You can't buy a home, and the lenders can't run their business!" Kumar said.

"CMHC guarantees the lender that if a buyer with a down payment of less than 20% defaults, the lender can sell the home, and if there is a shortfall in the amount owed to the lender, then CMHC will step in to cover the losses."

"That's a win-win!" said Kareena.

"Yes," confirmed Bibi. "The lenders are protected, and buyers can now buy a home with 5% as a down payment and enjoy the same interest rate as a buyer whose down payment is 20%."

"That sounds too good to be true," Kumar said.

"Well, there is a slight catch," Bibi said. "When a buyer's down payment is less than 20% of the purchase price, the lender will require the mortgage to be insured. To get a mortgage or home insurance, lenders must pay a premium to CMHC. The lender then passes that cost on to the buyer. CMHC sets the premium, which depends on the loan-to-value ratio."

"What's that?" Kumar said.

"That is the mortgage loan amount divided by the buying price," Bibi explained. "You can pay the premium upfront or add it to the mortgage amount."

"And how is the premium based on the loan-to-value ratio?" Kareena said.

"CMHC sets the insurance premium on a sliding scale," Bibi answered without missing a beat. "For example, if the down payment is 5%, the premium would be 4% of the mortgage amount. If the down payment is 15%, the premium drops to 2.8%."

"Wow!" exclaimed Kareena. I'm glad Justin referred us to you. Understanding mortgage financing is good information."

"There's more," continued Bibi. "The premium is also dependent on the purchase price. If the home costs $500,000 or less, then the minimum down payment is 5%, but if it is above $500,000, the minimum down payment is 5% for the first $500,000 and 10% for the remainder. CMHC can change the rules anytime based on the economy."

"That's like yin and yang," Kumar muttered. "On one hand, the premium helps buyers like us to buy a home, but on the other hand, the people with the smallest down payment, the ones who can't afford much else, pay through their noses."

"One last thing," Bibi said, sitting back in her chair. "I'm not sure if Justin mentioned this yet, but in addition to your down payment, you will need to put aside some money to cover the closing costs of buying a home."

"Let's take a break before we chat about closing costs," Kumar suggested. "You mentioned a pizza early on, and now I'm craving one. Any toppings you prefer, Bibi?"

Bibi smiled. "The pizza is here, Kumar. My manager took the liberty."

"You're one step ahead of us!" Kareena exclaimed, impressed with Bibi's service.

"If your agent—mortgage or real estate—isn't going above and beyond for you, are they the right fit?" Bibi countered. "That's why choosing someone experienced and with your best interests at heart is very important. Whether through pizza or securing a mortgage, I'm here for you. Now, let's eat."

"We have to write this down for reference," Kareena told Kumar on the way out. "There is no way we can remember all those figures she went through with us."

LESSONS LEARNED

- **GDS stands for Gross Debt Service. Total housing costs are divided by total gross income to arrive at that ratio, which is 32 percent of our gross income.**

- **TDS stands for Total Debt Service. It's the percentage of our gross annual income that we will need to cover all debts and loans, including our mortgage, and the cost of servicing the property and the mortgage. Once we zero in on the house we want, we will divide the total debt by our gross income, which should be less than 44%!**

- **CMHC stands for Canada Mortgage and Housing Corporation. They ensure high-value loans if the buyer doesn't have a twenty percent down payment.**

- **The broker will negotiate the best mortgage rate for us, but we must ensure everything is covered in the Agreement when we sign the mortgage papers.**

8 LEARNING ABOUT CLOSING COST

Bibi's wealth-building strategy–The Luggage.

While they enjoyed lunch, Kumar and Kareena revealed that they were expecting. Now, hunger satisfied, all three were ready to continue.

"By the way," Bibi said as she quickly cleaned off her desk. "Congratulations again! Having a baby is a pure bundle of joy. My partner and I made a significant purchase when I was pregnant without planning. It seems as though the soul sends its luggage ahead."

"You hear that, Kumar?" Kareena asked with a mischievous smile. "I don't know how much luggage our little soul will need."

"Well," replied Kumar, feeling empowered, "let's ensure we have a proper home to store that luggage. Bibi, what were you saying about closing costs?"

Bibi smiled at Kareena and Kumar's banter. "In addition to the down payment, closing costs are required when buying a home. These are the funds needed to transfer the house into your name. Closing costs vary from one transaction to another."

"What kind of costs?" Kareena said.

Bibi leaned forward. "The first thing you usually pay for is a home inspection. It is optional but recommended. A home inspection can cost a few hundred dollars for condos and much more for homes."

Kareena frowned. "My brother's wife's sister's daughter's husband is a building inspector, and I think he promised to inspect us pro bono. A dollar saved is two dollars earned."

Kumar's face brightened at the thought of potential savings. "We'll check his qualifications, and if he does it pro bono, even better," he agreed, hopeful about saving some money.

"Whatever the case be, just make sure he is properly qualified," advised Bibi. "You may save a few dollars hiring, but if the inspector overlooks something, it may cost you a few thousand."

"See?" Kareena said, nudging Kumar with her elbow. "I told you. We'll check his qualifications, and if he does it pro bono, even better."

Bibi leaned back. "Good! Now, next, financing can be complex. If your down payment is twenty percent of your purchase price or more, your credit is clean, and your income is good, it is inexpensive to finance. However, as we discussed, if your down payment is less than 20%, then the mortgage must be insured by CMHC. Remember, there is also HST on the premium."

"The government sure has their hands in every pocket," Kumar said.

"Kumar," Bibi interjected, "paying taxes is good. When you pay taxes, you also help the less fortunate. Think about health care, for example. It costs a lot of money that not everyone can afford."

"That's a good way to look at it," Kareena commented.

Bibi nodded. "Since your credit is clean and you have a solid down payment, we don't charge a fee. However, if you were self-employed or had blemished credit, we would need to borrow from a secondary lender, which can become expensive. A buyer can get caught paying mortgage broker, lender, and finder fees. In some situations, the buyer may need a first and second mortgage and the fees can escalate."

Kumar sat up. "Wait, how much are your fees?"

Bibi's words relieved Kumar. "There are no fees because the lender will pay us a commission," she reassured, easing Kumar's financial concerns.

Kumar let out a deep breath. "That's good news because we're trying to save every penny!"

"Saving pennies?" Kareena said with a quirk on her lips, ready to tease. "We've been doing that for a long time! I ate enough leftovers from the banquet hall. I guess we have to continue eating chicken chow mein."

"That's a delicious problem to have," Bibi said with a wink. "Keep in mind that lenders will need an appraisal done at the buyer's expense before lending. That usually costs a few hundred dollars, but we haven't gotten to the biggest cost yet—land transfer tax."

"What is that?" Kumar said.

"A property is a fixed asset and cannot be moved, unlike a television," Bibi explained. "As such, you cannot transfer ownership; hence, land transfer tax is payable to the government."

"So," Kumar said, "the government takes another piece of the pizza!"

"Exactly how much is that piece?" Kareena said.

"It depends on the value of the property. For example, the first $55,000 is half a percent in Ontario. From $55,000 to $250,000, it's 1%. From $251,000 to $400,000, it's at 1.5%, and the remaining balance up to two million is at 2%. I can't imagine you plan on your first house costing more than two million, but if you did, the tax would be at 2.5%."

Kareena did some quick calculations. "So, if we bought a house valued at, say, one million dollars, we would end up paying something close to twenty-nine thousand dollars in this transfer tax?"

Bibi smiled. "You're quick, Kareena. And accurate!"

"Wow," Kumar said, "I guess it's the price you pay for living in a progressive society!" Kumar thought for a moment before his face lit up. "Then we should buy a condo! There is no land to transfer!"

Bibi smiled. "In real estate, space in the air is considered land, so you still have to pay land transfer tax. You pay based on the purchase price. The higher the price, the higher the land transfer tax, and if you're buying in the *416* area code, then land transfer tax is doubled."

"Doubled?" exclaimed Kareena. "That's unbelievable!"

"Yes," agreed Bibi. "It can get costly. First-time buyers get a rebate of $4,000, but to qualify as a first-time buyer, you must have never owned a home anywhere in the world."

Kumar and Kareena exchanged a smile.

"We are first-time buyers," Kareena confirmed, "and we'd like to buy in Peel. That would help us save on land transfer tax. My parents live there, and they'll be helping with the baby." She rubbed her belly with a soft smile.

"Bibi?" Kumar said as he considered their options. "What do you think about newly built homes? Are those less expensive?"

Bibi tapped her fingers. "For newly built homes, additional charges include a new home warranty, education lot levy, grading fees, tree planting fees, and connection fees for water, gas, and hydro meters.

"Other hidden fees include the cost of a survey, builder's mortgage discharge fees, and deposit verification fees. You must pay for upgrades separately because you cannot add it to the mortgage."

Kareena leaned her head on Kumar's shoulder. "Let's stick to a resale."

"Lastly," Bibi continued, "you'll need a lawyer to handle the closing. Lawyer fees vary from one attorney to another. In addition to lawyer fees, remember that you will have to pay for disbursements."

"Disbursements," repeated Kumar. "I don't know what those are."

Bibi leaned forward to rest her chin on her hands. "Disbursements are money a lawyer pays for certain services like checking the title of a property, obtaining title insurance and property tax certificate, courier and photocopying charges. Always ask your lawyer for a statement of adjustment. It spells out how your lawyer uses the funds."

"How much do we need to put aside for the closing cost?" asked Kareena.

Bibi suggested putting aside 2% to 3% of the purchase price as a rule of thumb.

Kareena smiled. "Thanks for explaining the closing costs. I have one last question: I noticed a family photo behind you. How many children do you have?"

"Five!" Bibi exclaimed with a grin. "I'm not advising you to do this now, but there is one thing I'd suggest for the future."

"Is that for a home or the children?" Kumar responded.

"Both," Bibi said softly. "My partner and I used the equity from our principal home to buy another. I'm not saying to do this soon, but in time. At retirement, the rental income would be substantial. The best investment on earth is indeed earth."

After their meeting, the couple parted ways with Bibi. As they headed to their car, Kumar kissed Kareena on the forehead.

"First baby, first home. I guess we are getting the luggage before our baby arrives," Kumar said, playfully nudging Kareena.

"Well, we must get the house before the luggage!" Kareena countered with a playful laugh. "Come on, now that we know what we can afford, it's time to shop!"

Kumar said, "I'm looking forward to reviewing your notes tonight. All those figures have my head spinning."

LESSONS LEARNED

- The closing cost is within two to three percent of the purchase price.

- Building inspection will cost. Ask Bibi who she would recommend.

- Land Transfer Tax can hit us hard. Let's make sure we can cover the amount.

- Maybe Justin can help us find a reliable and reasonable real estate lawyer, but we must factor in the lawyer's fee and the so-called disbursements in the Closing Costs.

- We want to avoid taking a second mortgage, as we would otherwise pay high interest.

- I think we've decided to go for a resale — we don't have to worry about those closing costs for a new house, so we can forget about things like new home warranty, education lot levy, grading fees, tree planting and connecting fees for water, gas, hydro. Also no worry about survey costs, builder's mortgage discharge fees and that deposit verification fees.

9 SWEET DEALS & SMART MOVES

The $200K couch – lessons in real estate.

Kareena and Kumar met Justin at his office. Now that the couple had an idea of their budget, it was time to go shopping.

"Good morning!" Justin cheerfully greeted them. Today, we won't be seeing any homes. Instead, let's discuss a few things before going house shopping."

Kareena couldn't hide her disappointment. "I came prepared to look at homes. Time is ticking!"

Justin pulled out Kareena's chair for her before taking a seat. "There are a few more topics I'd like to inform you about before we start looking. For example, did you know you can buy a home without paying any land transfer tax?"

Kumar exchanged a wide-eyed look with Kareena. "That's a huge saving!"

Justin nodded. "I had a client, Cornelia, who bought a new home from the builder on a lease land. Since she did not own the land, there was no land transfer tax."

"Wow," exclaimed Kareena. "That's incredible!"

Justin shook his head. "When she bought the home from the builder, she had an option to buy the land for thirty thousand dollars, but back then, she couldn't afford it. I wish I had known her then because I would have advised her differently. Anyway, twenty-five years later, which is when I sold her home, similar properties without land leases were selling for $325,000. By then, the land value had gone up to $300,000. After paying for the land, real estate commission and lawyer fees, Cornelia walked away without any money."

Kareena gaped in shock. "I take that back," she said quickly, shaking her head.

"The point of this story," Justin continued, "is that there are two types of land lease—frozen and escalating. Frozen is when the land can be bought over within a certain time at a fixed price while escalating, which is like the one Cornelia had."

"We want to pay land transfer tax!" Kumar blurted out.

Justin leaned back with a gentle smile. "Now, I want you to imagine buying a home as a three-layer cake. The bottom layer is the largest, representing the location and having the most value.

"For example, an acre of land might be worth ten thousand dollars in Muskoka, a million dollars in Brampton, and ten million dollars in central Toronto."

Kumar nodded. "I understand the comparison," he said confidently, being a chef.

Kareena nodded alongside Kumar. "He made our wedding cake!"

"That's talent!" Justin responded. "Now, think of the middle layer as the size of the home. It's cheaper to upgrade a bigger home than to extend a smaller one."

"That leaves the third layer—the smallest one at the top," Kumar said.

Justin nodded. "That would be the upgrades. It's like the icing on the cake. While it makes the cake look beautiful, it doesn't add much substance. So, what have we learned?"

Kareena raised her hand promptly. "I know! When buying a home, look at the location, size, and upgrades."

"We are making progress!" Kumar exclaimed, high-fiving Kareena. "What else have you got for us?"

Justin smiled. "The next topic I want to explore is the principle of progression and regression."

"Progression is going forward, regression is going backward," Kumar said confidently.

"True, but in real estate, it's a bit different," Justin stated. "Progression is when the worst home on the block in an upscale area goes up because of the price of homes there. Regression occurs when the best home in a rundown neighbourhood drops in value due to the price of homes in that area."

"So then it's better to buy the worst home in an upscale neighbourhood than the best home in a rundown neighbourhood?" Kareena said.

"Yes," Justin confirmed. "Just remember, if you buy premium, you can enjoy premium–"

"And eventually sell premium!" Kumar said.

Justin smiled. "That's true, Kumar but I never sell properties I've bought. Instead of selling and moving up to a bigger home, it's better to increase the mortgage on your current home and use that equity to buy the next one. Then, you can rent your current home, and the rent received should cover the cost of the extra mortgage."

Kumar's eyes lit up. "I love that idea! We can become rich, Kareena. We'd be sleeping on the money!"

"We're already sleeping on the money," Kareena whispered to Kumar. "All the banquet hall tips under the bed, remember?"

Justin laughed. "I have to ask: Have you ever heard the story of the 200,000-dollar couch?"

"That's insane!" Kumar and Kareena blurted out together.

Justin shook his head as he leaned forward. "This couple had gone to a furniture store, seen a lovely couch, and bought it. Suddenly, compared to this beautiful new couch, all the other furniture in their home looked old. So, they decided to re-furnish the whole home. Once they bought new furniture, the house looked dated! So, they decided to renovate. When they finished renovating, their debts were through the roof, and they had to sell."

Kareena shook her head. "Sometimes we can get carried away, and before we know it, we're deep in the hole!"

Justin nodded. "Remember that you can change the light fixtures and the paint colours, but you cannot change the floor plan. When buying real estate, we should list our needs and wants and budget accordingly."

Kumar looked at Justin with concern. "We should buy a condo townhouse because it's much cheaper. I've been looking at some online."

Justin nodded. "While the current price difference between a freehold property and a condo townhouse is $200,000, you will pay condo fees if you buy the condo townhouse. Instead, I would recommend putting that extra money towards paying the extra mortgage on a freehold."

Kareena smiled and nodded. "If we buy a freehold property with an income potential, it would be cheaper to carry than a condo townhome."

"There's one last thing I want to mention," Justin said as Kareena and Kumar stood, thinking the meeting was over. "Avoid taking out any new loans or opening up more credit cards. Things like car purchases can wait until you move into your home. With more debts, lenders can disqualify you. Also, do not change careers midstream."

"Forget midstream!" Kumar joked. "We're not changing careers anytime soon!"

Justin reached out to shake their hands. "Thanks for coming today. Let's meet on Tuesday evening to see some homes. It's best to look at homes in the daylight, which we have much of this summer."

Kareena and Kumar headed for a Tim Hortons to discuss their lesson for the day over tea.

LESSONS LEARNED

- **While no land transfer tax is payable in Ontario on leased land, if we buy such a property, we should opt for a frozen lease rather than an escalating one.**

- It's cheaper to upgrade a bigger home than extend a smaller one.

- When looking for the right home, we should focus first on location, size, and upgrades.

- Progression is when the smallest home in an upscale neighbourhood increases in value because of the neighbourhood.

- Regression is when the best house in a run-down neighbourhood drops in value.

- The Red Couch Syndrome: Once we settle into our new home, let's concentrate on reducing the mortgage instead of buying expensive furniture.

- Let's forget about condos for the time being. Condo fees can be high. Instead of paying them, we can use the money to cover a higher mortgage on a freehold property with income potential.

- Starting today, let's avoid adding more debt to avoid impacting our credit rating. We should also stick to our current jobs to show stability.

10 CONDO PURCHASE 101

A baby shower turns into a real estate masterclass.

Kareena took a deep breath as Kumar pulled into a parking spot. Her sister, Preti, had organized a baby shower at her condo. Preti had a stunning penthouse suite with tall, sun-drenched glass windows and sparkling porcelain floors, furnished luxuriously.

"Have fun!" Kumar chirped before leaning over to kiss Kareena. "I'll pick us up some dessert. Tell Preti I said hi!"

"Thanks, Kumar," Kareena said as she got out. She waved him off and then took the elevator, already familiar with her sister's condo layout from previous visits.

She knocked on Preti's door, surprised when she entered and found she was the last one to arrive. After greeting everyone, she took a seat beside her sister.

Femi, a teacher and one of Kareena's friends leaned over to Preti and said, "I've just got to say, this condo is stunning! Did you buy it from the builder?"

Preti beamed in delight. "No, I bought it resale! Pre-built condominiums can take years to finalize, and I didn't want to tie up a large deposit with a builder paying only minimum interest. One major difference is that, unlike pre-builds, you see what you are buying."

Femi nodded. "I'm just asking because I want to buy a condo but don't know where to start."

Preti leaned forward and said, "I suggest looking at condominiums within your price range. Visit each building and compare suite sizes, maintenance fees and amenities. A modern building with great amenities will be more expensive, and the condo fees will be higher."

"That's great advice. You sound like a realtor," said Femi.

"I've been talking to Justin about this, too!" Kareena chimed in, wanting to share what she had learned. "Rundown buildings with dirty common areas will likely be less attractive to buyers, and the maintenance fees can climb with time because of all the repairs."

"Very true," Preti agreed. "An unattractive building with high condominium fees is a recipe for financial disaster since buyers won't want to buy there, and prices will plummet."

The girls were interrupted by a loud cheer. Kareena glanced over to see several of the guests clinking their glasses together.

"Why don't we grab some cake and head out on the terrace," Kareena suggested. "Preti has an incredible view."

They each got a slice and headed to the Toronto skyline balcony.

"I used to live in a mismanaged condo that required significant repairs. The reserve fund, money put away for future maintenance, had been depleted. Every owner had to pay $45,000 towards the repairs, which they called a special assessment," Preti said. "A special assessment is an unexpected fee that all owners in the building have to pay for major repairs or improvements. It can be a significant financial burden, so it's important to be aware of this possibility when buying a condo."

Femi gasped. "$45,000! What happens if you refuse to pay the special assessment?"

"Then the condo corporation can put a lien against your property. Add in lawyer fees—that $45,000 can jump to $50,000. They can eventually sell your suite under the power of sale," Preti said.

"That's why you should always research," Kareena said. "I remember before Preti bought this suite, she had her lawyer go through all the paperwork with a fine-tooth comb!"

Preti nodded. "With that special assessment in place, the condo prices dropped from $235,000 to $75,000. I remember sellers desperately trying to get out. while buyers avoided the complex."

"As an owner, won't I have any rights?" Femi said.

Preti finished her slice of cake, gently setting the plate on her outdoor table. "With condos, the unit owners usually elect a board of directors. The board looks over the affairs of the building. It's important as an owner to go to all meetings and be involved in the day-to-day operations."

"Are you involved?" Femi said.

Preti smiled. "I'm the current president of our board of directors."

"That's why she knows so much!" Kareena said.

Femi grinned. Thanks for your advice. That helps a lot."

"My pleasure!" Preti acknowledged. "Once you find the suite you want to buy, do your homework. Suites that overlook garage entrances and garbage pickup areas aren't as desirable and are more difficult to resell."

"Also," Kareena said, remembering Preti's former condo suite, "suites next to the elevator can be noisy. Look at the amenities, parking and locker before buying."

"How would I do that?" Femi said.

"Ask your realtor for a history of the suites sold in the building for the past year," Preti answered. "With that, you can establish what price to pay before you make an offer."

"Justin, my realtor, told me when buying a house to make my offer subject to financing and inspection," Kareena added. "Is that what you did, Preti?"

Preti nodded. "We had a third condition—obtaining and reviewing the *Status Certificate* from the condo corporation."

"*Status Certificate*?" Femi repeated, exchanging a confused glance with Kareena. "What's that? Does something need to be certified?"

"It's the DNA of the condominium," Preti explained. "The *Status Certificate* provides crucial information about the building. It has the bylaws and rules of the condominium."

"Is it so important to subject your offer to that, though?" Femi said.

Preti nodded and had a serious look. "I had a friend who bought a condo without any conditions and later discovered that the building was not pet-friendly. As a result, she tried to back out of the agreement. The seller sued for damages and won. Had my friend made an offer subject to reviewing the *Status Certificate,* she would have discovered that the building was not pet-friendly."

Femi looked up at the night sky in contemplation. "That's an expensive lesson."

Preti said, "The Certificate would include the condominium's most recent audited financial statement and a reserve fund study. It would also include other information, such as the breakdown of owner-occupied suites versus tenanted suites and whether the current owner is up to date with the condo fees. Financing on condominiums is more complex than financing on freehold properties because it hinges on the condominium's structural and financial status."

"Can I buy a condo with 5% as a down payment?" Femi said.

Preti stood up to stretch and helped her sister to her feet. "Well, if a buyer chooses to buy with less than a 20% down payment, the mortgage must be insured for the lender. CMHC is usually the primary insurer and would look at the building's financial health. Well-managed buildings with a strong reserve fund should qualify for buyers with high ratio mortgages."

"I've learned so much," Femi said, following the sisters back into the suite.

"Me too," Kareena whispered slyly. "Kumar and I aren't looking for a condo, but education never hurts!"

"I love your penthouse," Femi continued, "but this is beyond my stretch. I guess I have to start my search elsewhere."

Preti leaned forward, taking their plates from them. "There's a unit selling on the lower floor. It's vacant and needs some work if you don't mind renovating. I'm sure you can get it at a discount."

Femi lit up. "I'd love that! Kareena, I may have to borrow your realtor!"

Preti smiled. "I took a peek when it first came out on the market. The location is great, and the suite is spacious. It's away from the elevator, and the view is amazing. With a little cosmetic help, it's a step in the right direction. Instead of paying rent, you'll pay towards your property."

"Thank you both," Femi said. "I came for the baby shower and got showered with great advice," she joked.

"I'll give you Justin's number, and you can call him in the morning," Kareena said with a smile. "Now, let's get this party started."

Later that evening, lying in bed, Kumar said, "So Kareena, tell me. What lessons did you learn today from the visit to Preti?"

"Some valuable information we should keep in mind, even though we've already decided we're not interested in buying a condo at this time…"

LESSONS LEARNED

- While interest is payable on a new condominium deposit, the amount is small. The deposit is tied up until the building obtains condo status.
- Condo fees vary significantly with the amenities offered: the more amenities, the higher the cost.
- Condo suites overlooking garage entrances and garbage pick-up areas or adjacent to elevators can be problematic when reselling them.
- The Reserve Fund can sometimes not cover the significant repairs that are needed. When this happens, owners must supplement it with a mandatory *Special Assesment*.
- Condo rules are drafted and amended by a Board of Directors, and owners can run for a place on this Board to influence decisions.
- You can see the history of the condominium by asking for a *Status Certificate* from the Condo Corporation.
- In Ontario, buying a Condo with less than a 20% down payment requires mandatory insurance coverage through CMHC—Canada Mortgage and Housing Corp.

11 CONDO VS CO-OP: THE $200K PRICE GAP

There were two similar downtown suites, but one was $200,000 cheaper. Femi and her friends uncover the surprising truth about condos and co-ops.

Femi lounged on her sofa, scrolling through listings, when something made her sit up straight. Her eyes widened, and she gaped. Two stunning suites in the same downtown neighbourhood had caught her attention. Both had modern upgrades and identical amenities, but one was listed at $750,000, while the other was only $550,000.

Her heart pounded. "At $550,000, that's a steal!" she thought, dialling her friend Preti.

"Preti, I found these two incredible suites in the same area! But the one for $550,000 seems too good to be true. Do you think there's a catch?"

Preti barely hesitated. "That price screams bidding war. But there's no harm in checking it out. Kareena and I are at the spa—we'll meet you there at 4:00 p.m. Call Justin and set up an appointment."

By the time Preti and Kareena arrived, Femi and Justin were already outside the first building.

Justin greeted them with a warm smile as he held the door open. "This building is fantastic—spacious suites, plenty of amenities. The other one is just around the corner. Let's take a look."

When they stepped into the second building, Samuel, the owner, welcomed them. "Let's tour the suite first, then I'll show you the amenities," he said.

Kareena, pen and notebook in hand, turned to Femi. "This suite is just as gorgeous as the first one, but… look at the price."

Preti folded her arms, shifting her weight onto one leg. "Is there a catch?"

Justin nodded. "Yes. The first suite is a condo. This one is a co-op."

Femi frowned. "I don't get it. What's the difference?"

Justin explained, "In a condo, you own the suite outright. In a co-op, you don't own your unit—you buy shares in the building, giving you the right to live there. You're responsible for your mortgage, property taxes, and utilities with a condo. However, in a co-op, the entire building has one mortgage, one property tax, and shared utility costs. If another shareholder falls behind on payments, the others must cover the shortfall. Plus, since you pool the utilities, a larger household could end up paying less than its fair share."

Samuel, listening in, jumped at the chance to highlight the benefits of co-ops. "The strict board approval process means we get to choose our neighbours. We discourage renting, so there's a strong sense of community. Plus, co-op closing costs are lower—you don't pay land transfer tax or title insurance."

Justin smiled. "That's true, but financing a co-op can be tricky. Since you're buying shares instead of real estate, many lenders won't approve a mortgage for co-op purchases. Even if you find a lender, the co-op board can reject your purchase based on your financial plans. And when you're ready to sell, buyers must meet strict qualification requirements, making resale more difficult."

Preti turned to Femi. "Condos offer more financial flexibility. Thanks to CMHC insurance, you can buy with as little as five percent down. Plus, you don't need board approval to buy or sell. You control your mortgage, taxes, and utilities, which keeps costs predictable."

Justin nodded. "Unlike co-ops, condos are easier to finance and resell. They attract investors and are widely available in big cities. The trade-off is higher acquisition costs since you're purchasing real estate and paying land transfer tax."

Samuel said, "Buying condos is like investing in real estate, while co-ops are more like investing in stocks. With a condo, the property value typically increases over time. If the mortgage balance decreases and the building is well-managed in a co-op, your shares' value can also increase. Co-ops appeal to people who prioritize stability and community over financial flexibility."

Justin raised an eyebrow. "That's fair. However, condos have fewer restrictions and are generally better investments. When buying a condo, you investigate the building's financial health. When buying a co-op, they investigate yours."

Samuel smirked. "Co-ops may be harder to sell, but they offer a controlled environment. Shareholders make the decisions, so there's no risk of someone refinancing their unit irresponsibly."

Preti's expression turned serious. "In real estate, liquidity is key. Always buy what's easy to sell."

Kareena grinned. "I'm so glad I came. On the surface, salt and sugar looks the same, but deep down, they're completely different."

Femi let out a deep breath. She was slightly disappointed but relieved she had sought Preti's advice. "Lesson learned—there are no shortcuts in real estate. I'm lucky to have friends I can count on."

LESSONS LEARNED

- **In a condo, you own the suite. In a co-op, you own shares in the building.**

- **Co-ops require one monthly fee covering mortgage, property tax, and utilities.**

- **Condos: more straightforward to finance, buy, and sell.**

- **Co-ops have strict board approval, allowing control over who lives there.**

- **Co-op closing costs are lower since you're not buying real estate.**

- **Co-ops: generally cheaper than condos, harder to sell.**

- **Always invest in properties that are easy to sell.**

- **In real estate, there are no shortcuts.**

12 HOUSE HUNTING THRILLS

From bungalows to back splits, the couple explore the world of house shopping—until one house captures their hearts.

"*T*oday, we'll be navigating different types of homes!" Justin announced.

Kumar nudged Kareena in excitement. They were finally about to start house shopping.

"I can't wait!" Kareena said.

"Trust your instincts," Justin said with a smile. "The instant you enter through the front door, you'll know if the home is for you."

Arriving at the first home, Justin quickly scanned the property before gesturing to the driveway. "Do you guys see the potholes?" he asked, pointing them out. "The garage door looks worn, and the front door begs for a coat of paint. When you discover a few problems from the onset, the odds are there are more. Let's look at the inside."

Kareena was ready with her notebook and pen.

"I didn't even notice the garage!" Kareena whispered to Kumar as they followed Justin into the house. She made a note.

As Justin had said, the home needed extensive work. They moved to the following location, and when they arrived, Justin looked around.

"This home is a back split. The kitchen is in front, and a few steps lead to the upper level, where the bedrooms are. A few steps below is the third level. Some are side or front splits. These homes can have between three to five levels. They're ideal for families who value their own space."

Kumar scratched his head. "This home has two bedrooms on the upper and two on the lower floors. It's not the best for young families with little kids."

Kareena squeezed Kumar's hand. "Looking at it from another perspective," she said, "with this style, we can live in the upper two levels and rent the other two levels." She made a note in her pad.

"Absolutely," Justin agreed. "You're both right. That's why attention is important when choosing your home. Some split-level homes have three bedrooms on the upper floor. There are various types. I love the five-level back split type with the family room at the back, leading to a deck and the veranda in front."

"That sounds peaceful," Kumar admitted, "but I don't think this style would work very well for us at this stage in life. Maybe when the kids are older."

"Kids?" Kareena repeated, rubbing her baby bump.

Justin laughed heartily. "Let's head to the next one, then!"

They arrived at the next home, a one-story house with a more extensive driveway, a larger front garden, and a bright red door.

"This is like a home out of a fairy-tale book!" Kumar said, his eyes lighting up with excitement.

"Very picturesque," Justin agreed. "This is a bungalow. All the rooms are on the same floor. It's ideal for anyone who prefers everything on the same level."

Kareena shuffled through the home, taking in the space and unique layout. She had never been inside a house where the bedrooms and kitchen were on the same level. "We'd prefer a home with bedrooms on the upper floor. Kumar works nights and is a light sleeper," she said, and wrote in her notebook.

"That's great news!" Justin replied. "The more homes you see, the more you know what you want. We're narrowing our choices until we find your dream home!"

They cut through some cross streets and arrived at the next home.

Kumar stretched as he got out of Justin's car. "This is good learning. Some of these look different from the photos."

"That's why I always recommend coming out and seeing homes in person," Justin said. "Now, this is called a two-storey home."

Kareena smiled. "My friends told me that two-storey homes are great because families can live either upstairs or downstairs, and each tells its own story."

Justin burst out laughing. "I never thought about it that way. In real estate, it's a two-level home with a basement. The bedrooms are on the upper level. Most have the kitchen towards the back of the house. People like that arrangement because of the easy access to the backyard."

"I like this one," Kareena said to Kumar, and he nodded. "So far, it was the closest to what they sought." Out came the notebook from her bag.

It was a short drive to the next home. As they pulled into the driveway, Kumar's eyes lit up with recognition. "This is a detached home!"

Justin smiled broadly. "It may look like a detached, but don't be fooled because this is a link home."

"A link home?" Kareena repeated, looking around, puzzled. "I don't see anything linked together."

"You're right," Justin affirmed. "When the builder built these homes, they dug a trench and made a common footing around the perimeter. As such, outer basement foundation walls connect these homes. After construction, the builder put soil between the two homes, covering the foundation wall."

Kumar narrowed his eyes as he scanned the home before turning to Justin. "Real estate can be confusing. Does that mean that this is a link-detached?"

"Yes. It's linked at the foundation but looks like a detached home above the surface."

They left the house, continuing with their day. Justin drove into a small subdivision.

"Wow," Kareena said, as they pulled into the parking lot. "I don't think I've seen these kinds of homes before."

"These homes are small, detached homes," Justin explained, "but one side of the building sits on the property line. They're called zero-lot line homes. Since the home sits on the lot line, it becomes a part of the fencing for the other neighbour. If the owner needs to do any work on that side of the home, they must encroach on the adjacent property."

"I don't think I'd be comfortable with that arrangement," Kumar said, exchanging a concerned look with Kareena.

"It's not for everyone," Justin said before clapping his hands. "Let's move on!"

They drove to the next home.

"Townhomes?" Kumar asked when they parked.

"These are luxury townhomes," Justin said. "You'll notice that the roads are narrower and don't meet the guidelines for being considered a public road. There's also a little park in this subdivision. There is a monthly maintenance fee for maintaining the road and the park. The property is considered freehold, but a common road ties together all the homes. For that reason, they are called a parcel of tied lands."

"Looks like this is an intermarriage between a freehold and a condo," Kareena interjected.

Justin laughed. "You're a great student, Kareena. It's a mixture of both."

"This has been very informative," Kumar said as he stretched. "But I'm a bit tuckered out. Is there a lot more?"

"Our baby is also tired," Kareena joked as she rubbed her bump. "I can keep going!"

Justin joined Kareena in her laughter. "We have one more home to see today. Let's take a look."

Justin drove them to a detached two-storey home. The landscaping was impeccable, and the front garden had bright flowers and trim but well-maintained shrubbery. Justin unlocked the door and let them in.

Kareena's eyes darted across the home quickly, and she couldn't help but smile. "This is delightful!" she said, turning to grab Kumar's arm. "We can put our couch and TV in this corner!"

Kumar glided his hand along the granite counters. "I love the kitchen. There's plenty of counter space. I can prepare dinner and bake at the same time!"

"This home has three bedrooms, and the principal room comes with its own bathroom and walk-in closet," Justin added with a twinkle.

Kareena lit up with excitement. "Kumar, I think I'm having butterflies. This house is the one."

The couple proceeded to the basement which featured a walkout, an open-concept living and kitchen combination, a full washroom and a bedroom.

Justin opened the sliding door, allowing the couple to step outside. "It is a beautiful home, except the basement is not up to code. If you buy and plan to rent the basement apartment, it is imperative to apply for a permit and bring it up to code."

Kareena and Kumar nodded.

"You were right, Justin!" Kumar beamed. "The minute we walked through the front door, we fell in love with this home. It reminds me of when Kareena and I first met."

"Love at first sight," Kareena agreed, gazing adoringly at Kumar. She planted a kiss on Kumar's cheek. "Our baby is kicking. I think she likes it; that's a good sign. Let's buy this home."

Kumar froze before slowly facing Kareena.

"She?"

Justin laughed heartily, clapping Kumar on the shoulder. "Well," he chirped, "I guess some congratulations are in order."

That night, at the dinner table, Kareena pulled out her pad and completed her notes to discuss with Kumar.

LESSONS LEARNED

- **We must focus on our needs and keep those in mind as we look at houses on the market.**

- **The outside appearance of a house can reflect on the care taken inside—something to watch out for.**

- **A *Backsplit* can have three to five levels.**

- A *Bungalow* has all the rooms on the same level, which is uncomfortable for a family like ours, which needs some peace at the end of the day.

- A *Link- Detach Home* is linked in the basement but looks like a detached.

- A *zero-lot home* is on the lot line, and part of the fence separates it from the adjacent house. The neighbours are also granted an easement to enter the yard.

- Townhomes come in many types. A Freehold provides your own private backyard and you're responsible for the upkeep, same as the house.

- When we buy, if we intend to rent the basement, it's essential to have it finished by a reputable builder and with a building permit to bring it up to municipal code.

13 SEALING THE DEAL: IT'S LIKE TYING THE KNOT

From negotiations to signing on the dotted line to a few surprises.

Justin pulled into the office, and Kareena and Kumar were in tow. They had just finished touring the home and were ready to draft an offer, so Justin suggested they return to discuss the terms.

"When I met my wife," Justin said as he parked, "it was love at first sight. We had some things in common, but we had to meet each other halfway on the uncommon ones. Eventually, we did tie the knot. Buying a home is similar, I like to say. First, you find the right home, then negotiate with the seller, and, finally, the contract."

"Let's call the seller and negotiate a price!" exclaimed Kareena, excited to get the ball rolling.

Justin smiled. "In real estate, an offer is a legally binding contract known as an *Agreement of Purchase and Sale.* It must be in writing for it to be valid. Many things must be considered when making an offer, such as the price, the deposit, what the price includes, and the closing date."

"What price should we offer?" queried Kumar, sharing a look with Kareena.

"I found that similar homes are selling for five thousand below what the seller is asking," Justin said as he gathered some papers in a folder and handed them over. "Here is a market analysis of the area. In a market with more buyers than sellers, buyers will try to outbid each other with multiple offers. With multiple offers, sellers tend to consider offers with the highest price and strongest deposit without any conditions such as financing or inspection."

Kareena shook her head. "That's not right. Buying a home is an expensive venture. We need to arrange financing and conduct an inspection."

Justin nodded. "The good news is that we have a pre-approval already, and the sellers have done a pre-inspection and are willing to share the report. We can give the seller an unconditional offer if there are multiple offers. If we buy without any conditions and the lender's appraisal value is lower than the purchase price, we must pay extra money to cover the difference."

After a lengthy discussion on their terms, Kareena and Kumar asked Justin to draft and submit an offer of fifty thousand below the current listed price with two conditions: one for financing and the other for inspection. This condition for financing allows the buyer to secure a mortgage within a specified period, usually a week or two after the offer acceptance. If the buyer fails to secure the mortgage, the offer becomes void. The second condition is to allow Kumar and Kareena to conduct a home inspection to ensure that the property has no significant defects.

"I'll walk you through what I'm drafting so you'll both be familiar with the process," Justin said, gesturing for them to sit on his side of the desk to view the agreement. "The first part of this contract has the buyer and seller's names, the address and the legal description of the property.

"Next, we have the price you want to offer." He pointed out the sections as he described them. "Then we have the deposit."

"Deposit as in our downpayment?" asked Kumar. "I thought we would give that to the bank!"

"No," Justin clarified. "Deposit in an *Agreement of Purchase and Sale* is the money you will give with the offer. It varies from one transaction to another."

"So the seller holds on to our money?" Kareena asked.

Justin shook his head. "No, normally, the deposit is held in trust at the seller's brokerage for both parties during the transitional period. A strong deposit is between five and ten percent of the purchase price. It shows goodwill and the buyer's financial strength."

"That's good," Kareena said. "We can put in a strong deposit."

"Now," Justin continued, "every offer has an expiry date and time, which is the *irrevocability date*. That means the person making the offer cannot revoke the offer until the expiry time. The transaction becomes binding if the other party accepts the offer during that time frame. Buyers should endeavour to make the irrevocability period as short as possible. If it is long, the sellers can wait closer to the expiry time, hoping that other offers might come in and, in so doing, ignite a bidding frenzy. A reasonable time frame is between twelve to twenty-four hours."

"That reminds me of Preti, Kareena's sister," Kumar said, nudging Kareena mischievously. "She would give you something and take it away with the same breath. Next time, I will tell her that her offer needs to be irrevocable."

Justin laughed at the comment. "You learn something new every day! Now, let's talk about chattels and fixtures. Chattels are personal items not attached to the property other than by their weight, such as a fridge, stove, washer and dryer. Anything connected to the property is known as a fixture and belongs to the property. When you sell a property, the ownership of the fixtures goes with the sale, and the seller cannot remove it."

"Is there a way to definitively say whether something is a chattel or fixture?" Kumar said. "I'm sure some items might be confusing."

Justin nodded. "Usually, to decide if something is a fixture or chattel, a twofold test is used: one, the extent to which the object has been attached, and two, the purpose for which the item was attached. If the item is a fixture, such as a light fixture, and the seller wants to remove it, it should be in writing in the offer as an exclusion. If not, then it goes with the property."

"How about a garden shed or rose bushes?" quizzed Kareena.

"The roots fix rose bushes while a garden shed rests by its weight," Justin replied. "The rose bushes are fixtures, and the garden shed is a chattel. Sometimes, it can become confusing, so I like to say: *When in doubt, spell it out.*"

"I like that!" Kumar exclaimed. "When in doubt, spell it out."

Justin nodded. "Next are rental items. There are many instances when sellers rent the furnace, AC, hot water tank and other items. If a buyer assumes the rental contract, asking for a copy before committing is important," he advised.

"What about title search?" asked Kumar. "Who is searching for what?"

"Well," Justin said, "there is a timeline called the requisition date for the buyer's lawyers to review the history of the property to confirm ownership and discover if there are any claims or liens against the property. This is called a *Title Search.* Usually, that date is set two weeks before closing, but lawyers usually research the title in advance and even at closing to see if there are any new changes."

"Titles!" Kareena said. "I always relate titles to books, movies and things like jobs. I'm a teacher, and Kumar is a chef. I guess each property has its title."

Justin said, "That's right, Kareena. Let's look at the *completion date.* The completion date is when the buyer pays the seller the remainder of the money, and the seller, in turn, transfers ownership to the buyer. It must be on a business day when the registry office is open.

"If there are any other things we want to add to the agreement, they are listed under various schedules. For example, in our *Agreement of Purchase and Sale*, we have clauses stating that the offer will become void if we do not secure financing or are not happy with the home inspection. In this section, we also ask for a survey of the property if it's a freehold."

After drafting the paperwork, Justin reviewed everything again before Kumar and Kareena signed the agreement. Once everything had been signed, Justin contacted the seller's realtor, and the negotiating process began. It took a few back-and-forth discussions and counteroffers, but eventually, everyone agreed.

Back home, Kareena was elated when Justin called to tell her the good news. When she got off the phone, she couldn't help but smile. She quickly found Kumar and gave him a big hug. "We tied the knot on our purchase!" she said.

Kumar blinked in disbelief. "We made it?" It took a minute for the confirmation to sink in, and his eyes lit up.

"We made it!" he repeated, sharing Kareena's enthusiasm. "Turn on the barbeque, honey; let's celebrate!"

After dinner, Kumar and Kareena sat down to recap their discussion with Justin.

LESSONS LEARNED

- We signed the Agreement of Purchase and Sale to make an offer. It's legally binding, so I'm happy that our agent, Justin, reviewed all the clauses with us.

- The *Conditional Offer* we made for financing and inspection will protect us if we run into obstacles from the bank or if the house has defects we haven't seen up front.

- Thankfully, we took the time to obtain *pre-approval* for a mortgage, which will speed up the process and give us high confidence.

- Our deposit, thankfully, is protected since it's held in a trust account by the broker.

- Chattels are items not attached to the property. Fixtures are more or less connected to the property and included in the sale.

- I hope the seller owns all the items in the house, but we have to decide whether we are prepared to take over a lease if some items, like the furnace, water tank, and air conditioner, are not.

- Our lawyer will search the title at the registrar to ensure we get a clear title for the house when the deal closes.

14 A DETAILED INSPECTION RESULTED IN BIG SAVINGS.

Louisa's expert eyes and guidance during the inspection gives the couple valuable insights.

Bibi met with the couple soon after they made the purchase.

"Congratulations!" she said as soon as she saw them. "Your mortgage has been approved, and the appraisal came in at the purchase price. If you haven't done so already, you can now arrange an inspection of the home."

Kareena called Justin to give him the good news. "Bibi said we can go ahead and do our inspection."

"Amazing!" Justin replied. "I'll make the arrangements and meet you at the home."

The day soon arrived for the home inspection. Justin met them at the property, and beside him was a middle-aged woman with a bright smile.

"Kareena, Kumar," Justin greeted them, introducing them to Louisa. "She's an excellent home inspector. Stick with her, and you'll learn a lot today. I guarantee it!"

Louisa shook their hands. "Nice to meet you both. Let's start from the outside and work our way in. As you can see, a few hairline cracks exist along the foundation.

These cracks occur because concrete contracts and expands over time. Sealing these cracks is essential since they can widen over the winter. We'll check for water leaks in the basement later during the inspection, but I want to inform you."

"That's good to know," Kumar whispered to Kareena as Louisa surveyed the outside of the property, taking endless photos. "Did you bring your notebook? I feel like today's going to be full of information."

Kareena pulled out her notebook and pen.

"Well," Louisa said, placing her hands on her hips. "The landscaping is good. Notice how it slopes away from the foundation? That's what you want. The eaves troughs have long extensions discharging water away from the home. If water lodges near the foundation, it might eventually seep into the basement. Let's tackle this roof."

Kareena looked at Kumar, mouth agape. "Are you going to climb it? That's dangerous! Kumar, you go up and help her!"

Louisa laughed heartily. "While I appreciate the thought, don't worry." She went to her vehicle, and her drone hovered above the house within thirty seconds, snapping photos. Louisa calmly inspected every angle of the roof with a joystick and a computer screen. At one corner, a few shingles were missing. "It's a fairly new roof, but we need to replace the missing shingles," she noted.

Kumar and Kareena observed Louisa meticulously inspect the external GFI outlets, the lights, the driveway, and the garage, seizing every opportunity to point out minor defects and corrective measures. Kareena made her notes as they went along, confident in the thoroughness of the inspection.

"A home is like a person, each with its unique problems. We are looking for major issues while educating the buyers about minor ones," Louisa explained. "I may be pointing many things out, but not everything is a problem or issue. As a homeowner, there are some things you should be aware of that you may not know. There may also be some stuff that isn't a problem yet, but you should keep an eye on it."

Kumar emphasized the value of their presence during the inspection. "Our friend suggested we could receive the report via email and not be present. But I'm glad we didn't follow that advice. Being here and seeing everything firsthand is invaluable."

"You mean your brother," Kareena said, nudging Kumar. "I'm glad we didn't listen to him."

With the outside done, Louisa steered them to the finished basement. She flashed a light on the external walls and used a moisture meter to check for dampness. "The basement is dry. That's good news. The cracks are not leaking," she said before inspecting the fuse box. "There are some fuses that are double-tapped here. Usually, it's one wire per fuse. Double tapping indicates that someone other than an electrician did some electrical work. It's important to conduct an electrical safety audit," she suggested.

Justin massaged his chin. "Electrical fires are dangerous. We'll need to arrange with the seller to fix that."

Louisa took out her infrared camera, checking for uninsulated areas in the basement and pest infestation. "This home is well insulated. There are a few minor air leakages around the windows. Here's the main shut-off valve for water. It's essential for an emergency, such as a burst pipe; this valve is the shut-off valve for the outside water. It's wise to turn off the outside water and drain the pipes in the fall to prevent freezing. When water freezes, it expands and can rupture the pipes."

"Shut off pipes in the fall," Kareena noted the information.

Louisa turned her attention to the furnace, AC, humidifier and thermostat. "The furnace is like a second set of lungs. Change the filters regularly. It's good to clean the air ducts. During winter, the furnace will extract moisture from everywhere, including our skin. Have the humidifier serviced and operational. It will prevent dry skin and shrinking floors," she advised.

There wasn't much more to inspect in the basement. The four proceeded to the main floor, and Louisa photographed the serial numbers on all the appliances.

"We know what the fridge and stove look like," Kumar said as he watched Louisa snap another photo.

"This can become handy if you think the seller may have switched the appliances before closing. I put everything in my report, so you can always go back and verify information if you aren't sure."

"That's why she's the best," Justin affirmed.

Louisa finished with the kitchen, opened all the taps, and flushed the toilets while checking the water flow.

"It's important to clean the drainpipes often. You can use a drain cleaner, baking soda, vinegar, and then run some hot water. Now, let's take a look into the attic."

"That's the scariest part," Kumar confided to Kareena. "Anything could be up there."

Louisa used a small ladder and hobbled her way up. "You'll need to add some insulation, but the attic is dry and mould-free. Usually, when there is poor ventilation in the attic, the warm air eventually condenses on cold spots and falls, causing mould to flourish."

The entire inspection lasted about three hours. Louisa provided the couple with a list of deficiencies.

A few days later, after receiving the report, Justin began renegotiating the offer for the seller to correct some of the shortcomings or compensate the buyers on closing.

Justin and the seller's realtor agreed, and Justin prepared an amendment removing the conditions for financing and inspection. The parties agreed to a price reduction so that Kumar and Kareena could correct the deficiencies once they became the owners.

Once everything had been signed and settled, Kumar and Kareena could wait for the closing date. Soon, they would be proud homeowners.

LESSONS LEARNED

- Hiring an experienced and qualified Home Inspector.

- Check the following areas:

  - Basement walls (especially for cracks and moisture).

  - The roof for missing tiles.

  - Electrical panel for overloading and other unprofessional flaws.

  - Note the serial numbers for appliances.

  - Attic insulation should be up to standard and mould-free.

- Items to place on our ongoing maintenance list:

  - Change the filters for the furnace and humidifier often.

  - Shut off external water and drain taps in the Fall.

15 BUYING A NEW HOME WITH JOHN AND MARY

Explore the hurdles of purchasing a newly built home, from hidden costs to essential upgrades.

It was a sweltering summer Sunday. Femi and Preti had visited Preti's friends, John and Mary, who had purchased a newly built home two years prior. The closing was finally approaching. John and Mary had already signed off on the pre-inspection and had received their keys just a few days earlier. It had been a long wait, but they were ready for it. Kareena volunteered to join them, bringing her notebook and the extensive notes she'd compiled from her experience.

Femi loved the idea of purchasing a newly constructed home. She considered the lengthy closing period advantageous because it allowed her to save more for the down payment, but she wasn't familiar with the process. After discussing with Preti and Kareena, they decided that a conversation with John and Mary would be beneficial.

Upon arrival, John led the trio on a tour of the minimally furnished home. As they walked, he emphasized, "Before making a purchase, it's vital to investigate the builder's reputation thoroughly. If any neighbours are already living there, talk to them and hear their thoughts on the builder. Also, check with the Canadian Home Builders Association to confirm if the builder is a member. Consider the builders' after-sale service and what the warranty covers."

Mary, an architect who had worked for the builder, shared her insights as they explored the house. "When buying new, it's important to think long-term. Consider the next five to ten years. Will your family structure change? Think about additional parking and potential lifestyle changes. Seniors might prefer a bedroom and a full bath on the main floor, while a young couple might be planning to start a family. Choose a location that suits your needs, and always consider school and commuting time. The next step is to take a realistic look at your financing."

Femi nodded, absorbing all the advice. "It's a beautiful home," she said with a smile. "The design is perfect, featuring high flat ceilings, oversized windows, and a double door entry. Can you tell me more about purchasing a new home?"

John and Mary exchanged a serious look. "Unlike resale, new home purchases can be daunting," John said. "Hidden costs, such as development fees, deposit verification fees, mortgage discharge fees, education lot levy, builder's lawyer fees, new home warranty fees, water, gas and hydro meter fees and many more, cannot be added to the mortgage. All of this is in addition to the down payment."

Preti, looked at Femi. "If you're considering a new build, being cautious is crucial. Unlike newly constructed condominiums, purchasing freehold properties doesn't typically have a cooling-off period. However, some builders might allow buyers a forty-eight-hour window. Make sure the contract is conditional upon your lawyer's approval."

Femi nodded as they entered the kitchen. She couldn't help but glide her hands along the marble countertops. "I love the upgrades. We visited the model home, and it's a replica of yours."

Mary smiled. "As an employee of the builder, I received some benefits," she admitted. "Most people love the model home because of the upgrades. Budget carefully and choose only the most important upgrades. Builders typically make the most profit on these extras. Opt for upgrades that are easy and cost-effective to implement at the time of purchase, such as higher ceilings, larger basement windows, and separate entrances for the basement. Upgrades like thicker carpets and granite countertops can wait. Keep in mind that banks will finance the property at its base value and may not cover the costs of upgrades. The closing costs and upgrade expenses may ultimately become out-of-pocket costs."

John said, "When buying new, expect delays. Builders will provide adequate notice in the event of a delay. The contract may have a *critical date;* if the builder misses that date, the buyer can agree on the closing and seek compensation or opt out of the deal. Approximately one week before completion, the builder will schedule a pre-inspection. We just had ours."

"John also works for the builder as a subcontractor," Mary continued. "During the pre-inspection, check if the home has the same plan you choose and look for imperfections and defects. I've seen new homes without insulation in the attics, unanchored toilets, and missing towel racks and dryer vents. It's crucial to have homes inspected by professional home inspectors. After the inspection, the builder will provide you with an inspection sheet to sign, indicating that you've reviewed the home and are satisfied with everything except the defects noted in the statement. If you overlook something and the warranty doesn't cover it, the builder can refuse to fix it."

Femi took a deep breath. "It feels like new home purchases are a roller coaster adventure that can be both exhilarating and exhausting, but with careful planning, they can be the most rewarding. I'm getting butterflies."

Preti shook her head in amusement. "Take your time, Femi. It's a significant step and a lengthy journey ahead."

"I know," Femi replied. "But the journey of a thousand miles begins with the first step. Kareena, what are your thoughts?"

Kareena pulled out her notebook. "I can only read the notes I've taken over the last few months, but everything I heard today confirms what I've heard so far."

LESSONS LEARNED

- **Items to check for the builder and property:**
  - ○ **Is the builder a member of the Canadian Home Builders Association?**

- o Are there loosely installed items or defects in the equipment?

- Only include upgrades that are necessary and which can be covered by the mortgage.

- Unlike newly built condominiums, freehold properties don't have a legal cooling-off period unless granted by the builder.

- Expect delays in the completion of the project and plan alternatives.

- Budget for hidden costs connected with buying a new home, including Development Fees, Mortgage Discharge Fees, New Home Warranty Fees, and any other items that can be added later but won't be covered by the mortgage

16 PAVING THE WAY FOR A SOFT LANDING

From avoiding last-minute pitfalls to unexpected turns, Kumar and Kareena gain valuable insights from their family.

"*I*n India," Kareena's father, Pawan, explained, "I gave thanks daily, but here I kept all the thank-you's for today!"

Parbatie, Kareena's mother, cracked up in laughter. "Is that why you were up since four thanking people?"

She had risen early that morning to begin cooking. The sheer amount of cooked goods had transformed their dining room into a mess hall. After a decadent lunch, the family rested in the living room.

Once the murmurings had quieted, Kareena announced, "Kumar and I bought a home. There were a few issues with the inspection, but Justin, our realtor, negotiated a reduced price for us." She tapped her fingers. "We can go shopping for furniture. Leons has had a no-money-down deal for two years."

"You don't want to do that," said Preti. "Lenders usually check your credit before closing. If there are any significant changes to the borrower's credit, they can withdraw their mortgage commitment. Any financing purchases, such as furniture or cars, should be postponed until closing. Applying for a loan or accumulating more debts before your deal closes is not advisable."

"I did make a note of that, but I thought, since we accepted an offer, it should be safe," Kareena said.

Parbati shook her head and reclined her chair as she closed her eyes. "Not so. Also, you should notify your landlord that you'll be moving soon. Usually, it's sixty days from the end of the term."

"What if they're on a month-to-month tenancy?" asked Preti.

"Then it's sixty days from the end of the month. Don't forget to book the elevator."

Kareena smiled serenely. "We already gave our notices, booked the elevator and arranged movers," she said with a hint of pride.

"What we don't have yet is a real estate lawyer for the closing," Kumar said, reaching out to squeeze Kareena's hand. "Though I'm not sure why we need one."

"The closing occurs when you transfer money from the buyer to the seller, and the lawyers transfer the deed from the seller to the buyer," Preti explained. "In a mortgage, the deed is transferred to the lender as security for the loan. The buyer would then possess a document known as a *Transfer Deed*. Your lawyer would handle the paperwork to facilitate this process."

"Don't forget you also need home insurance," Preti said. "It's a requirement from the lender, and your lawyer would need it when closing. It protects you against damages to the interior and exterior of the home if someone is injured on your property and for loss or damage of your personal belongings."

"I will call our auto insurance company," Kumar told Kareena. "We can negotiate a bundled deal at a discount. I'll get a few quotes."

"That's a great idea!" Pawan piped up. "Parbati, you should call the insurance company. We can also get a bundle!"

Parbati glanced at Kareena. "You have plenty of old gold jewellery. Put things like that and important documents into a safety deposit box."

"What about mortgage insurance?" Preti said.

"We opted for it," Kareena confirmed, "but they didn't explain it to us."

"Mortgage insurance is called a decreasing term insurance," Preti explained. "In death, the insurance company will pay the remainder of the mortgage. Instead of mortgage insurance, some people choose a level term insurance for twenty-five years. In the event of death, the family gets the full payout. They decide how to use it."

Kumar nodded. "Let's keep this option until closing. It costs nothing; if something happens before closing, the surviving partner will be mortgage-free. We can cancel the policy when the deal closes and take a level term."

Kareena rubbed her stomach gently. "I still need to inform the utility companies and arrange a transfer," she mentioned quietly.

Preti said, "That's a good idea. You should also inform everyone about the change of address. Have the post office forward any mail with the old address to your new one. It costs a small amount, but it's better to be safe. Also, remember to update your driver's licence."

"When we bought this house," Parbati said, "we arranged a walk-through before closing."

"Yes," Pawan said. "That is the best time to confirm that the owners completed whatever work they were supposed to do. Double-check that the home you bought is in the same condition as when you finalized the contract. I don't know if the home you bought has tenants, but if it is, you should confirm that the property is now vacant."

"Oh yes!" Parbatie exclaimed. "Pawan is right. If the tenants are still there and the deal closes, they become your problem."

"The sellers live there," Kumar said. "Our agreement allows for two visits. We're going for our first visit next week and hope to meet the owners. They're downsizing and plan to leave us some furniture and lawn-care equipment."

"Don't forget to bring two pieces of valid ID when you see your lawyer to sign all the papers," Preti advised. "When I bought my condo, my driver's licence had expired. We ended up asking the seller for an extension. It was an expensive lesson because the seller needed the money from us to close their other home. I had to cover all their losses, including movers, lawyers and other penalties."

"Thank you for the advice," Kumar said, overwhelmed with everything they had learned. As they parted ways from the family, Kumar teared up. "Your family is the rainbow in our cloud."

Kareena wiped his tears and smiled joyfully. "Yes, honey, I know, but you are the rainbow in *my* cloud."

She pulled out her notebook. "Let's make time tonight to go through our checklist."

LESSONS LEARNED

- Don't take on additional debt before closing the sale—it will impact your credit rating.

- If you're renting, be sure to give enough notice to the landlord—for example, in Ontario, it's sixty days from the end of the term if you're on a lease and sixty days from the end of the month if you're not.

- Necessary: engage a real-estate lawyer for the closing to ensure everything goes smoothly.

- You must take out home insurance on the new house—the lender requires it—and negotiate a package deal that includes the car.

- Mortgage Insurance provides coverage for paying off the mortgage if circumstances dictate. It can also be converted to long-term coverage.

- Send the address change to your contacts and arrange mail forwarding by the post office.

- Arrange for pre-closing inspections of the house you purchased.

17 CLOSING DAY VICTORY WITH SUSIE TANG

With expert advice, the young couple's lawyer overcame last-minute surprises along the road to homeownership.

As the closing date approached, Kumar and Kareena liquidated most of their investments and transferred them into a new account designated solely for housing. Bibi called early one Saturday morning to check in on them.

"I just verified with your lender," Bibi said, "and everything is okay with the closing date for next Monday. Your first house, your first baby—it looks like the stars are aligning for you."

Kumar and Kareena couldn't be more excited for the weekend to pass. Their realtor had organized a final walkthrough at the property later that day.

Suzie Tang, the lawyer recommended by Kareena's parents, contacted Kumar and Kareena and instructed them to prepare a bank draft for the amount needed to finalize the purchase. This amount represented the balance of the down payment due at closing. Suzie also recommended that Kumar and Kareena obtain a fire insurance binder naming the mortgage bank as the *Loss Payee*. "A fire insurance binder is a temporary insurance policy that provides proof of insurance coverage until a permanent policy is issued. It's a crucial step in the closing process as it ensures that the property is protected against fire damage, which is a requirement for most mortgage lenders."

The meeting was set for Thursday, four days before their closing date.

Suzie was a well-dressed professional in her thirties, with shoulder-length hair and oversized glasses. Suzie smiled and welcomed Kumar and Kareena to her office. "I looked into the property's title and discovered a third owner listed on it."

"But we only have two sellers listed in the agreement!" Kareena exclaimed, attempting to avoid panicking at the thought of a third, unfamiliar seller.

The lawyer reached over and gently squeezed Kareena's hand. "It's one of the seller's aunts, who passed away two years ago. If she were alive, she could have objected to the sale. However, as the aunt was a joint property owner, upon her death, her ownership passed on to the sellers as the surviving owners."

"Don't scare us like that," Kumar said, putting a hand to his chest and taking a deep breath.

Suzie tried to calm them with a smile. "This is why a title search is so important. If the aunt had owned the property as a tenant in common, her share of the property would have gone to her estate. That could have created a headache, as the aunt's estate would have needed to be one of the sellers."

She continued and explained the significance of *Title Insurance*. "Title Insurance protects against third-party claims on the property that may arise after the deal has closed, such as outstanding property taxes, work orders from the city filed against the property, and claims of ownership by other parties. Moreover, the lender will not allow the transaction to close unless Title Insurance is in place to safeguard their interests."

The terms of the mortgage and the *Mortgage Disclosure Statement* were then discussed. This document from the lender primarily outlined the total interest paid and other costs associated with borrowing the money over the mortgage term.

She went on to explain, "As the buyer's lawyer, I represent you and the bank lending the money. I must share any information you provide with the bank while equally representing your and the lender's interests. This role ensures that your interests are protected throughout the process. You will need to provide me with proof that both of you have paid the loan and the credit cards before the closing date "

Suzie Tang showed Kumar and Kareena another document. "This is the buyer's *Trust Ledger Statement*. It is a document I prepared and serves as a record of all receipts and expenditures at closing. There is a column for debit and another for credit. We know the full amount owed to the seller, which is in the debit column. The debit column includes other expenditures, such as land transfer tax, title insurance costs, and legal fees and disbursements. The credit column contains the mortgage amount to be forwarded by the lender at closing and the amount for the bank draft you provided for the remainder of the down payment. The total of the debit column, representing all expenditures, and the total of the credit column, reflecting all the funds I have received from you and the lender, should be equal.

"According to the sales contract, the closing deadline must be no later than six pm on the closing date. The closing relies on different individuals completing multiple tasks, which, once finished, would align seamlessly. Initially, the lender transfers the mortgage funds to my law firm's trust account. This is a crucial step as it ensures the necessary funds are available for the transaction."

Suzie had already prepared various certified cheques based on instructions from the vendor's lawyer, including payments to settle the seller's remaining mortgage, property taxes, and any other liens on the property. "I will also forward the closing funds to the seller's lawyer, who will hold the money in trust. The seller's lawyer will then release the Transfer/deed to me, and I will register the ownership Transfer/deed and mortgage electronically.

Suzie continued, "Many gears are turning all at once before completion. Once we transfer ownership, you can get the keys." Suzie then brought out another document. "This is a *Statement of Adjustments*. I received it a few days ago. The seller's lawyer prepares this document. The statement includes a credit in favour of the seller for the purchase price and a credit to you for the amount of the deposit you made when you signed the *Agreement of Purchase and Sale*.

"There's an adjustment for property taxes. The seller has paid the property tax for the entire year and will receive a credit for the remainder of the year from the closing date. Additionally, there is an adjustment credit in favour of you, the purchaser for any amounts the seller owes. Finally, after accounting for the various credits, you'll see at the end of the statement, the amount of money I will send to the seller's lawyer."

The lawyer told Kumar and Kareena that the furnace and central air conditioner were rental items, and the rental company registered a lien against their title. According to the *Agreement of Purchase and Sale*, the sellers had agreed to acquire the equipment at their own expense before closing. Suzie informed the couple that they received a credit on the statement of adjustments. She intended to use that credit to pay off the furnace and central air conditioning after closing and secure discharges of the liens on those items.

"I've arranged for the movers to come to our apartment in the morning of the closing date so we can move into the new house by three pm," Kumar told Suzie.

Suzie nodded. "I hope the transaction will be closed by then, and you'll have the keys. However, there's no guarantee that the deal will close by three. Please remember there can be many unexpected delays. I might not receive the mortgage funds from the bank until late afternoon on the closing date, or the seller's lawyer may not be available to finalize the transaction until later. You might not receive the keys and be able to move into the house at three pm."

"What should we do?" Kareena asked, sitting up with attention.

"I recommend that you arrange for your movers to come in the afternoon and move your belongings to the new house by six pm on the closing date. If you go to the home by six pm, you will have sufficient time for the transaction to close, and you don't have to wait with your moving truck. I strongly advise changing the locks once you've moved into your home, as you do not know who else may have a copy."

As they listened to Suzie's advice, Kumar and Kareena learned that anything could happen until the very last minute in real estate.

"In real estate," Suzie said, as she walked Kumar and Kareena to the door, "the deal is never done until it is done. You both have a restful night's sleep, and we'll connect on Monday."

Monday arrived quickly, and everything went smoothly. However, their mortgage funds did not reach Kumar and Kareena's lawyer's trust account until 3:30 p.m. Suzie had to rush to her bank to prepare the certified cheques for the closing and courier them to the seller's lawyer's office.

Fortunately, the seller's lawyer received the funds at 4:40 p.m. The electronic registration of the transfer/deed and mortgage was completed just before 5:00 p.m., which was the cut-off time for the electronic registration of the documents.

After confirming with the seller's lawyer, Suzie called Kumar and Kareena. "Congratulations—you are now the proud owners of a lovely home! Fortunately, you delayed your moving time, saving you extra moving costs. Additionally, the sellers may still move their household items when you arrive at your new home with your moving truck. While they are supposed to leave by six pm, it's always better to cooperate and work together to finalize the move."

Kumar and Kareena didn't mind giving the sellers extra time to move out. They sat one last time on the balcony of their apartment, taking in the scenery.

LESSONS LEARNED

- *Title Insurance* shows third-party claims against the property—items like property taxes and liens.

- The *Mortgage Disclosure Statement* lays out all the terms and conditions set by the financing institution.

- The buyer's *Trust Ledger Statement* is a comprehensive report on all receipts and expenditures to close the purchase/ sale.

- The *Transfer/ Deed* is the final document validating the property's ownership transfer to the buyer.

- The *Statement of Adjustments*, prepared by the seller's lawyer, shows an itemized list of all transactions relating to the sale of the property.

- Plan and prepare for all eventualities from a delayed closing, including the impact on movers and additional costs.

18 REAL ESTATE FRAUD: VALUABLE INSIGHTS

With identity theft climbing, Kareena and Kumar learn how to protect their home.

It was winter in Toronto. Pawan and Parbati longed for some sunshine and wanted to escape, but Pawan felt anxious. He had read an article about a family returning home from vacation only to discover that someone had impersonated them and sold their house.

"Imagine going away on a trip, and when you return, you discover that an imposter sold your home and the new buyers have already taken possession. You've lost your home and all your personal belongings. This incident happened to a homeowner in Etobicoke," Pawan said, alarmed.

Parbati began biting her nails. "A home is personal; in many cases, it has lifelong memories. For many, it represents their entire life savings. Selling a home is complex and involves numerous steps. So how exactly did the fraudsters manage to pull it off?"

Pawan shook his head, recalling the article. He had read about two individuals who posed as homeowners and hired a realtor to sell the property. Months later, the real owners returned. "The fraudsters used fake identification. It had been all over the news."

"Let's call Justin and see what he thinks," Parbati suggested. She wanted a vacation but was now concerned about leaving their home for an extended period.

Justin welcomed them warmly and listened to their concerns. "Well," he explained, "when selling a home, a realtor must cross-reference photo identification, such as a driver's licence or a passport, with the owner's name from the land registry. It can be challenging for a realtor to determine fake documents. Identity theft is becoming more prevalent given that most information is online."

"What can homeowners do to protect themselves?" queried Pawan.

"Fraudsters are on the lookout for easy targets. In the story, the impostors knew that the homeowners were away, simply breaking in and looking for information. Many snowbirds leave their homes unattended during their absence. If you plan to be away, ask a close friend, family member, or house sitter to keep an eye on things. Investing in a reputable security alarm company is also worthwhile," Justin advised.

Parbati nodded, her smile slowly returning as she cheered up with Justin's advice. "We are not worried about that. We have many family members to watch our home when we leave."

"That's good!" replied Justin. "It's also a requirement of your insurance that your house be taken care of while you're away. For instance, the insurance company could invalidate your policy if you have a water leak that isn't detected until you return home.

"Fraudsters also examine your social media profiles. We often share our experiences with friends online during family vacations. For many of us, social media is an open book for a fraudster to read. Be sure to monitor your social media profile, and when you're away, avoid exposing it," he cautioned.

Pawan chuckled. "Parbati is a Facebook queen." He nudged her playfully. "Everything she does is on Facebook."

"Stop it," Parbati hushed Pawan, embarrassed.

"I guess we will only post photos of our vacation when we return home," Pawan said. "Instead of during our vacation."

"Fraudsters also target mortgage-free homes," Justin continued. "When a property has a mortgage, it is registered on the title, or history, of the property. Transferring the property to a different owner is more difficult because the lender must consent. Lenders have sophisticated security systems set in place to detect fraud. For fraudsters, it means more hoops to jump.

"A mortgage-free property is a prime target. If you are mortgage-free, open a home equity line of credit. When this happens, the lender is on the property title. You can ask the lender to keep it locked. If you need to use it, you and the lender can unlock it together," Justin advised.

"That's not a bad idea," agreed Pawan. "We don't have to use the funds if we don't need to."

"Fraudsters target the elderly, often focusing on those who live alone. They pose as friends, gradually building a relationship over time. As this relationship deepens, so does the trust of the older adult. In many cases, this has even led to marriage, particularly if the victim lacks close family or friends to warn them. The fraudster often becomes a joint owner of the property. It's wise to consider adding a family member to the title of your home.

"Children should closely monitor their elderly parents and help them manage their finances. You must secure important documents like SIN, passport, and banking information safely."

"We are not at that stage yet," Parbati said. "But it would be a good idea to add Kareena later."

"We'll think about it, Justin," Pawan agreed. "What else would you suggest?"

"Freeze your credit," Justin said. "It's free and straightforward. To do so, contact each of the two credit bureaus: Equifax and TransUnion. They will provide you with a PIN for future use."

"What about our credit score?" Pawan asked.

"This won't affect it," Justin responded.

"How times have changed," Parwan lamented. "I wish we could return to the good old days when there were no computers and no internet."

"Hah!" Parbati lampooned. "You can go back to your cow-cart days. I love my Facebook and TikTok."

"One last thing," Justin interrupted before they could continue. "Use two-factor authentication. Hackers are using sophisticated systems to gain access to your computers and accounts. Two-factor authentication — 2FA— gives another level of security. For example, if someone signs into an account with a password, you will receive a text message with a code you need to enter to gain access."

Justin explained that selling someone's home without their consent is quite unusual. The fraudsters would have first needed to steal the owner's identity and then access the property for viewing. Later, they would have to be vetted by a lawyer, who would settle any liens and mortgages on their behalf. Ultimately, after the sale, their lawyer would deposit the funds into the owner's account or prepare a draft in the owner's name.

Justin continued, "Since the imposters pretended to be the owner, they likely had to open an account in the owner's name and withdraw all the funds. The point was that many things had to align to pull this off.

"With easy access to information, cunning hackers, AI and scam artists, identity theft is rising. Many people are buying identity theft protection services. These help to catch potential fraud early, but they cannot protect us from fraudsters," explained Justin.

After they got off the phone Parbati told Pawan, "The best protection is to safeguard ourselves."

Pawan nodded and clasped his hands together. "With that solved, let's get packing!"

LESSONS LEARNED

- Going away? Take the following steps:
  - ○ Don't publicize the event on social media.
  - ○ Leave your house looking *lived-in* with lights on, timers, etc.
  - ○ Engage a house sitter to visit the property.
  - ○ Stop deliveries and newspapers.
- Arrange a Line of Credit, and the financial institution provides a first line of defence since it has a lien on the property.
- Consider adding a family member to the title of the property.
- Freeze your credit through Equifax and TransUnion.
- Use Two-Factor Authentication (2FA).
- Explore purchasing an identity theft service.

19 HOMEOWNERSHIP & PARENTHOOD— A JOURNEY

Kumar and Kareena learn how to turn their dream home into a future foundation.

Kumar and Kareena's hearts raced the following day as they relaxed in their new home. Their priest, Omkar, was on his way. Femi and Preti had prepared delicious meals for the occasion, and Pawan and Parbati had gathered everything needed for the priest to bless their home.

After prayers, Kumar and Kareena packed a few boxes with sweets. They visited the neighbours, handing out the goods and their contact information with cheerful smiles. Their neighbours would become an extended family, and they wanted to make good impressions, fostering a sense of community and connection.

Sebastian and Lizzy—Kumar and Kareena's friends arrived early. Lizzy, who was at the end of her second trimester, was energetic.

"We brought smoke and carbon monoxide detectors!" exclaimed Sebastian, proud of the thoughtful gift. "It's recommended that they be replaced every two to three years, and the batteries should be replaced twice yearly."

"Most fires begin in kitchens and laundry rooms," Lizzy chipped in. "It's smart to have smoke detectors in these areas."

Justin stopped by. "I have new locks for your doors. One of the first things to do when you buy a home is to change your locks. You never know who else may have a spare key," he stressed.

"Thank you, Justin," Kumar said, clapping him on the back. "I never thought about that. Security is paramount."

"Congratulations on your purchase!" Bibi exclaimed, appearing behind Justin and holding a bottle of champagne. "I arranged with a duct cleaner to clean the air ducts, which is important, especially for those with allergies. When you move into a home, one of the best things to do is to clean and sanitize the vents. Remember to replace the furnace filters every other month."

Louisa—Kumar and Kareena's home inspector, took the sweets Kareena handed out to her as she explained the importance of knowing where the water shut-off valves were located.

Louisa munched on the sweets and explained: "Water, unlike many other liquids, expands when frozen and can burst the pipe. Water can cause major damage and mold infestation in a house quickly. It's important to turn off the outside water taps when you turn on the heat,"

She removed the cover from the sump pump before pouring water into it. The pump turned on automatically, and Louisa smiled. "Test the pump this way every so often. If there is heavy rainfall and the pump is not working, the basement can flood," she advised.

When they returned upstairs, they saw most of the company sitting in a circle on the floor, engaging with each other.

When Bibi saw Kareena and Kumar appear, she clapped. "How many weeks make a month?"

"Four," answered Kumar.

"How many months are in a year?"

"Twelve," answered Kareena.

"If there are four weeks in a month and twelve months in a year, then, logically, the year has forty-eight weeks," Bibi continued.

"What happened to the other four weeks?" asked Lizzy.

"When you pay a monthly mortgage, you make twelve equal payments. That is equal to forty-eight weeks. Ask your lender to change your payment structure to accelerated payments," Bibi advised. "With accelerated payments, you are making thirteen monthly payments instead of twelve in a given year. If you make accelerated biweekly payments, which is slightly higher than half a month's payment, you can take away close to five years of payment on a thirty-year mortgage.

"Mortgage is a blend where a portion of the payment goes towards interest, and the remainder goes towards paying down the principal. With every payment, the principal reduces slightly. The next payment is calculated on the lower principal, meaning the interest payment is slightly smaller. Since the payment is the same for each installment, you will add a bigger portion to the principal over the long run. Add one or two hundred dollars to the regular payment to deflate the principal."

Kareena frowned. "We were hoping to save and pay down the mortgage by the allotted ten percent once per year on the anniversary date."

"It's best to divide that amount and pay it biweekly instead of once yearly," Bibi replied. "This way, you can make many small chops to the outstanding balance instead of a lump sum yearly payment. It's the reverse of compound interest."

"A little axe can cut down a big tree," Sebastian teased.

Susie Tang called to check in with Kumar and Kareena. "Now that you are homeowners, you need a Will. I can prepare one for you at half the price," the lawyer said.

Dr. Sayeed arrived with Maggie, the retired investor from the old folks' home, around 4 p.m.

Dr. Sayeed chuckled. "I promised Maggie dinner today and decided to bring her here. This way, I can hit two birds with one stone."

"The buffet is still warm!" Kumar said.

Maggie savoured the sweets. "Congratulations on your purchase! I remember the first home I bought. After seven years, I took some equity from that home and invested in a second one. After another seven years, I took some equity from the first two and bought two others. Seven years later, I used the equity from the four homes to buy four more. In twenty-one years, I bought eight properties, each rented for $2500 per month. The rental properties gave me a yearly income of around $240,000. That's better than any RRSP or other pension plan."

"Maggie is correct," Bibi agreed, getting up to fix Maggie a plate. "She's right to focus your mind on the bigger picture. Real estate is a good investment over the long term. The trick is paying the mortgage and using the equity to buy other properties."

Kareena got up to help but felt a sharp pain. "Kumar!" she said as the others crowded around her to help her to her feet. She grabbed Kumar's arm shakily. "Kumar, I think I'm having contractions!" She shook him. "Grab our *go bag*; it's time—our baby is coming!"

Dr. Sayeed stepped in, helping to support Kareena as Kumar ran around the house, grabbing various items. "Let's go to the hospital," he cheered. "Maggie, I'm sorry, my dear, but—"

"I'll drop her back," Bibi said. "Maggie, I'd love to pick your mind on more matters. No use letting this food go to waste; let's grab some more and get comfy."

Kumar escorted Kareena to the hospital. Their bundle of joy was about to arrive. Buying a home had been a good idea. It would provide shelter for the family and, with time, become the springboard to building wealth.

Parenthood was a book by itself.

While Kumar cradled their new baby in his arms the following day, Kareena pulled out her notebook and made her final notes.

LESSONS LEARNED

- **Install Fire Alarms and Carbon Monoxide detectors.**
- **Change door locks if a repurchase.**
- **Arrange for an air-duct cleaner.**
- **Create a House Maintenance List:**
  - **Changing furnace and humidifier filters.**
  - **Shut off the water in the Fall.**
  - **Test the sump pump if one is installed.**
  - **Other items need constant maintenance.**
- **Arrange for accelerated payments for the mortgage.**
- **Contact a lawyer and prepare a Will.**
- **Prepare a long-term real-estate investment plan.**

20 INSPIRING FRIENDS TO PURSUE THEIR DREAMS

With co-ownership options, the couple shows their friends how to turn financial challenges into opportunities.

How time flies! It had been a whole year since Kumar and Kareena became homeowners, and they loved every moment. They no longer hauled grocery bags through narrow hallways or waited endlessly for the groaning old elevator. Still, nostalgia tugged at their hearts as they returned to their old apartment building to visit friends who hadn't yet taken the plunge to home ownership.

The moment Kareena stepped into the lobby, a wave of emotion hit her—this was her first home in Canada, where she made many memories. The walls still smelled faintly of spice and takeout, and the flickering fluorescent light above the mailboxes hadn't changed.

As they squeezed into the rickety elevator, it lurched and groaned on its way up, each floor announced by a tired, reluctant *ding*. Kumar chuckled. *Some things never change.*

When the doors finally creaked open, Cindy and Robbie greeted them with warm hugs. They were also eager to buy a home, but the numbers weren't on their side yet.

Kareena had anticipated this conversation, so she had asked Justin, their trusted realtor, to stop by, thinking there may be a way to turn their friends' dreams into reality.

The four friends sank into the couch Kareena and Kumar had passed down—a relic of better days, now fraying at the edges like their patience with apartment living. Justin took a seat opposite them.

Cindy leaned forward, her fingers drumming against her knees. "With sky-high rents and the cost of living, owning a home isn't just a dream—it's a myth."

Kareena gave Cindy a gentle hug. "Where there is a will, there's a way. Let's hear what Justin has to say."

Justin leaned in, eyes alight. "Co-ownership. Instead of wasting money on rent, two or more families can buy a place together and split everything. It's catching on in cities like Toronto." Justin's eyes sparkled with enthusiasm. "Think about it—combined incomes make mortgage approval way easier. Pooling resources? That means a bigger down payment and lower monthly costs. Both families split the mortgage, property taxes, repairs—everything. And here's the best part—over time, you build equity together and leverage it to buy a second property."

Robbie frowned. "What happens if the parties cannot get along?"

"Co-ownership has its perks, but it's not all smooth sailing," Justin admitted. "If one owner has major debt, bad credit, or a low income, it can tank the mortgage application for everyone. Then there's the financial risk—if one person falls behind on payments, the rest must cover the slack. And let's not forget the everyday logistics—who's shoveling snow at 6 in the morning? Who's mowing the lawn? Splitting a home means splitting responsibilities, which can get messy quickly." Justin folded his arms." Co-ownership thrives when everyone pulls their weight. It's a game-changer, especially in tight-knit communities where families team up to buy a home. The fewer partners there are, the better—too many hands in the pot can mean trouble. The key? Everyone chips in for the down payment and closing costs, and before signing anything, they lay out exactly how they'll split the space, the bills, and the responsibilities. No surprises, no drama—just smart investing."

"Co-ownership is like a marriage—with a prenup," Kumar said. "Before signing anything, you need an exit strategy. What happens if one partner dies? That's where the ownership structure comes in."

"You've got two options," Justin added. "Joint tenancy or tenants in common. Joint tenancy is like 'til death do us part'—if one owner passes away, the other automatically inherits the entire property. It's common for married couples or partners who want their share to go directly to the other.

"Most co-owners go for tenants in common—where each person owns a specific percentage of the property based on their investment. If one partner dies, their share goes to their estate. Unlike joint tenancy, where everyone gets an equal slice, tenants in common let you tailor ownership to match what each person puts in."

Kareena said, "It's all about planning—because real estate and surprises don't mix."

"That's correct," said Justin. "Think of a co-ownership agreement as your blueprint. A real estate lawyer should draft it, covering everything from living arrangements to finances. A co-ownership agreement has two parts: a cohabitant agreement and a property agreement."

Kumar nodded. "The cohabitant agreement states who lives where and how shared spaces work. Treat it like a rental setup—maybe one owner takes the basement while the other gets the upper floors, splitting costs accordingly. The other contract, a property agreement, addresses title ownership and what happens if someone wants out or can't pay their share."

Robbie suggested that the co-owners set up a joint account for mortgage payments, utilities, and upkeep and keep three months of reserve in the account. "This way, we do not have to worry about surprises."

Justin continued, "Choose a partner who complements your strengths and someone you can trust wholeheartedly. If your partner is married, be aware of how their relationship with their spouse can affect them and, by extension, you."

Cindy sat up. "Co-ownership offers compelling advantages that far outweigh the risks. Robbie and I know the perfect family two doors down."

Kareena squeezed Cindy's hands gently. "When you factor in the money saved on rent, the equity you can accumulate, and the significant savings on shared expenses, it's clear that co-owning is a savvy financial move."

Justin added, "It's not just about owning a piece of property—it's about building wealth while minimizing costs."

After bidding their friends and Justin goodbye, Kumar and Kareena pulled up at a Tim Hortons.

"Kareena, we bought a home already. Why are you still taking notes?"

Kareena smiled. "Maybe one day, I can use this information to help another family."

Kumar became emotional, "You have all the qualities to become an amazing realtor."

LESSON LEARNED

- Co-ownership of a home is a viable option for those struggling with the high cost of homeownership. It offers combined resources for a larger down payment and easier mortgage approval.

- Shared responsibilities in co-ownership require precise planning and communication to prevent misunderstandings.

- Financial risks exist in co-ownership, especially if one party defaults or has poor credit.

- Before co-owning a property, you must agree on space, finances, and responsibilities.

- Two types of ownership structures exist: joint tenancy (equal shares, automatic inheritance) and tenants in common (customizable shares based on investment).

- Having a cohabitant agreement and a property agreement drafted by a real estate lawyer helps ensure fairness and clarity in the partnership.

- Setting up a joint account for payments and keeping a reserve fund can mitigate surprises.

- Trust and compatibility between co-owners are essential, especially when family dynamics are involved.

- Co-ownership can be a smart financial strategy, building wealth while sharing costs.

GLOSSARY OF TERMS USED IN THIS BOOK

ACCEPTANCE: when a buyer agrees to purchase a property under conditions set by the seller.

AFFO: *Adjusted Funds From Operations*. It's arrived at by taking the Net Operating Income used in the FFO and adding the non-cash flow items like depreciation and non-operating gains like the gains from the sale of assets.

AGREEMENT FOR PURCHASE AND SALE: legal contract between a buyer and seller outlining the terms for purchasing a property.

APPRAISAL: an estimate of the property's value based on what similar properties recently sold for. With an assessment, you can calculate the equity in the property. A licensed property appraiser would research the property through MLS (Multiple Listing Services).

ASSIGNEE: an individual or entity receiving property or title under the terms of a contract.

ASSIGNMENT: the transfer of property rights from an assignor to an assignee. Contracts often permit the assignment of pre-construction condominium units.

ASSIGNOR: the individual or entity conveying property or title under the terms of the contract.

BDLM: Broadloom Where laid;

BUYERS REPRESENTATION AGREEMENT: a written contract between a buyer and a Real Estate Agent outlining the terms of their working relationship.

CAP RATE: *Capitalization Rate*. The rate of return the REIT is providing for shareholders.

CHATTELS: property not permanently attached to the land or building and can be moved.

CLOSING COSTS: the cost linked to the purchase or sale of a home, such as sales tax, lawyer fees, lender fees, and down-payment.

CLOSING DATE: the date when ownership/title and money change hands. Many steps must be taken simultaneously to reach this point in the transaction.

CMHC: Central Mortgage and Housing Corp [a government agency in Canada]. Protects the lender (institution financing the mortgage) in high-ratio mortgages. The cost of the premiums is rolled into the mortgage. CMHC insurance can be avoided by making a down payment of at least 20% of the purchase.

COMMISSION: a fee paid to an employee for a service or transaction performed. When selling a home, for example, the seller will pay a commission to the Realtor involved in that transaction.

CONDITIONAL OFFER: an offer to purchase depending on certain conditions being met.

CONDOMINIUM (CONDO for short): a building in which the units are individually owned, but common areas, such as the roof, passageway, elevators, etc., are jointly owned.

CONDO FEES: Condo owners pay monthly fees for maintenance, heating, lighting, and access to facilities like a swimming pool or fitness room.

CO-SIGNER: someone guaranteeing the payment of a loan.

CREDIT REPORT: a report generated/ obtained from an approved Credit Reporting Agency, laying out the creditworthiness status of the person(s) in question.

DEED: a legal document regarding the ownership of property.

DUE DILIGENCE (PERIOD): The buyer's lawyer usually has a time frame for researching the property's title. This period is known as the due diligence period, and the deadline is the requisition date.

EASEMENT: is a right of use (on a property) given to someone other than the homeowner.

ELF: Electrical Light Fixtures.

EQUITY: the value remaining after deducting the amount owed on the mortgage from the current sale price of the home.

FFO: *Funds From Operations* and represents the actual cash flow from the REIT.

FINANCIAL PLAN: a plan drawn up to show the proposed income and expenses of a particular business undertaking. Might be prepared for a Financial Institution as a loan prerequisite.

FLIPPING: purchasing and selling a property with the primary objective of utilizing and profiting from the upturn in market forces.

FREEHOLD TOWNHOUSE: the owner wholly owns the property, including the land.

GDO: Garage Door Opener.

GDS: Gross Debt Ratio. The ratio of the cost of running a house to Gross Annual income. Helps the lender determine if a homeowner can afford the cost of running a home.

HELOC: Home Equity Line of Credit. An amount of credit extended by a financial institution with a portion of the equity in your house registered as collateral.

HOME INSPECTION: a process of inspecting a property to determine its flaws. Typically undertaken by a purchaser who will engage a professional.

IRREVOCABILITY CLAUSE: the deadline set for the offer/ acceptance of the sale/ purchase of the property

LAND TITLE REGISTRY: a government agency that transfers the property's title from the seller to the buyer.

LAND TRANSFER TAX: a sales tax paid when purchasers buy real estate. Since a buyer cannot move the land (like other products such as a computer), it can only be transferred to the new owners. As such, it is called land transfer tax. It is calculated based on the sale price of the property.

LEASED LAND: where the tenant owns the building, but the landlord retains title to the land.

LIENS are registered claims against the property. They represent unpaid debts, such as property taxes from a previous owner or unpaid amounts for services performed on the property, such as installing windows or a furnace. Many contractors employ this method to guarantee payment for work done.

LINKED HOUSE: "A link detach." The foundation walls below ground are connected by two common walls running lengthwise along the entire stretch of homes. The cross-foundation walls are then constructed, and the earth is thrown between the homes. Above ground, it looks detached, but below it is linked.

MLS: Multiple Listing Service, where properties are listed along with the values.

MORTGAGE: the outstanding balance due on a loan secured to acquire property. Also, SECOND MORTGAGE: loan granted by a second institution or person.

MORTGAGE DISCLOSURE STATEMENT: This statement includes all the terms and conditions set by the financing institution, including items the buyer had to take care of, like liquidating loans and credit cards.

MORTGAGE INSURANCE: provides coverage for paying out the mortgage if circumstances dictate.

MORTGAGE PAYMENT: the amount due in a specific agreed-to period as payment to the institution that financed the property purchase. Typically made up of principal plus interest on the outstanding balance. Interest is generally calculated as a more significant portion of the payment, with a smaller amount going towards the principal in the early years, and the ratio of principal to interest switches as the years accumulate.

MORTGAGE PREAPPROVAL AND PREQUALIFICATION: when a buyer is prequalified, it's only an estimate of how much she can afford. It does not investigate the finer details, such as her credit and ability to pay. On the other hand, PRE-APPROVAL imposes such responsibilities where the buyer completes an application and all the necessary documentation for review. If successful, the lender would issue a commitment letter to the buyer.

NET WORTH: total assets minus liabilities, as calculated on a Balance Sheet. Represents the amount of ownership in assets.

OFFER: is an agreement to purchase a property under specific conditions. This agreement is time-sensitive and contains deadlines.

PRE-INSPECTION: During the pre-inspection phase, the home is investigated for imperfections and defects that need to be adjusted before taking title.

PRE-QUALIFIED: an estimate of how much a lender is willing to lend for a purchase.

PROGRESSION: when a run-down home in the neighbourhood is favourably impacted by other homes in an upscale neighbourhood and increases in value. SEE ALSO REGRESSION.

PROPERTY INFORMATION STATEMENT: a disclosure statement that the seller may have provided to the realtor. A history report can also be requested, providing information on whether the home ever had an insurance claim for fire, flood, or sewage back-up or if the property was used as a grow-up.

RATE OF RETURN/ RETURN ON INVESTMENT: a measure of whether proceeding with an investment is worthwhile. Calculated as the net gain or loss on an investment over a specified period, expressed as a percentage of the investment's initial cost.

REGRESSION: when the best home in a run-down neighbourhood drops in value due to the impact of other run-down houses.

REIT: Real Estate Investment Trust. This is a way of creating a diversified real estate portfolio without actually buying a property.

RESERVE/ RESERVE FUND: the amount set aside as a contingency (by Condo Boards, for example) for a specific purpose or unexpected expenses. Required by law in some jurisdictions.

RRSP: Registered Retirement Savings Plan (in Canada). An amount allowed, within specific parameters, by the Federal Government as a deduction to arrive at your taxable income. If allowed, it is most likely to be called something different in other jurisdictions.

RRSP MORTGAGE: where the investor (in the RRSP) converts his RRSP into a mortgage on a specific property. This is called a private mortgage, and the financial institution and the RRSP holder negotiate the terms and conditions.

SECOND MORTGAGE: a mortgage taken out on a home that already has a mortgage (see MORTGAGE above). There are specific rules governing which mortgage has priority.

SECURED LINE OF CREDIT: a loan obtained from a financial institution and secured with real property, such as a home. The cost of borrowing is generally lower than that of a conventional loan. (SEE ALSO HELOC).

SELLER TAKE BACK MORTGAGE: a private mortgage where the seller lends the money for the purchase directly to the buyer. (SEE ALSO MORTGAGE).

SHORT TERM RENTAL: rental of a property for less than a year, typically not covered by a lease. Companies such as Airbnb engage in such rentals.

SPECIAL ASSESSMENT: This is an extra cost a condo owner pays in addition to monthly maintenance fees. For example, if the parking lot needs repair and there is not enough money in the reserve fund to cover the cost, every owner must contribute to cover that extra cost. Failure to pay may result in a lien being placed on the unit.

STATEMENT OF ADJUSTMENTS: an itemized list of all transactions relating to the property sale.

STATUS CERTIFICATE: the By-laws and rules of the condominium corporation.

STRESS TEST: a financial test designed to determine how much a buyer can afford if the interest rate increases—whether they can fetch the heavier financial burden with the same income level. Some governments impose this test when the housing market accelerates, increasing house prices.

SURVEY: As in a Land Survey, the boundaries of a property are laid out.

TDS: Total Debt Service: the percentage of gross annual income needed to cover all debts and loans,

TFSA: Tax-Free Savings Account (in Canada). Money set aside in an approved account, accumulated likely from tax-free income and not subject to tax on withdrawal. Conditions govern the operation.

TITLE INSURANCE: a type of insurance policy that protects the homeowner from some losses regarding transferring title; can be purchased at the time of transfer of title to the new owner.

TITLE SEARCH: a process where a lawyer searches the land registry to determine the titled owners of the property.

TOWNHOME: a residential property usually attached to other (town)homes in a row.

TRANSFER DEED: This is the final document validating the property's ownership transfer to the buyer. At this stage, the house keys are turned over.

TRUST LEDGER STATEMENT: a comprehensive report on all receipts and expenditures on closing the purchase/ sale.

TWO FACTOR AUTHENTICATION: a security method requiring two forms of identification to access an account.

ZERO LOT HOME: where the house is built against the following property, leaving no space between the home and lot line.

INDEX

Z

JAY BRIJPAUL BSc, FRI

Jay Brijpaul is a dynamic author, successful realtor, and passionate community leader whose life and career are testaments to perseverance, vision, and dedication. In his first book, *Wealth Through Real Estate Investing,* Jay delved into financial success and personal growth principles, offering readers practical strategies for building and sustaining wealth. His insightful guidance is rooted in real-life experiences, making his teachings relatable and actionable.

In the world of real estate, Jay has earned a stellar reputation as a top-tier realtor. With almost four decades of experience, he has helped countless families find their dream homes and investors achieve significant returns. His deep understanding of market trends and a client-first approach have made him a trusted name in the industry. Jay's commitment to excellence and integrity has set a benchmark for aspiring realtors.

Beyond his professional achievements, Jay is a dedicated community leader who believes in the power of giving back. He actively participates in various philanthropic activities, focusing on initiatives uplifting the underprivileged and fostering community development. His leadership and volunteerism have positively impacted many lives, reflecting his unwavering commitment to social responsibility.

Jay Brijpaul's journey from humble beginnings to becoming a respected figure in wealth creation, real estate, and community service inspires many. His work is driven by a profound belief in empowering others, helping them realize their potential and achieve their dreams.

ALSO FROM MIDDLEROAD PUBLISHERS

MiddleRoad | Publishers

www.middleroadpublishers.ca

Making Literature See The Light Of Day

**ALL BOOKS AVAILABLE AT AMAZON
WORLDWIDE.
eBook versions available from all eBook
channels**

www.kenpud.wordpress.com

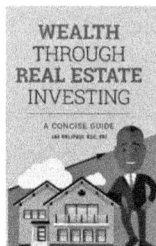

WEALTH
THROUGH
REAL ESTATE
INVESTING

A CONCISE GUIDE

MiddleRoad|Publishers

www.ingramcontent.com/pod-product-compliance
Lightning Source LLC
Chambersburg PA
CBHW060035210326
41520CB00009B/1138